Pitman
Education
Library

EDUCATION AND
CONTEMPORARY SOCIETY

EDUCATION
AND CONTEMPORARY
SOCIETY

BY

H. L. ELVIN

Director, University of London Institute of Education

PITMAN PUBLISHING

First Published by C. A. Watts & Co Ltd 1965
First published in this
edition 1973

Sir Isaac Pitman and Sons Ltd
Pitman House, Parker Street, Kingsway, London WC2B 5PB
PO Box 46038, Portal Street, Nairobi, Kenya
Sir Isaac Pitman (Aust) Pty Ltd
Pitman House, Bouverie Street, Carlton, Victoria 3053,
Australia
Pitman Publishing Company SA Ltd
PO Box 11231, Johannesburg, South Africa
Pitman Publishing Corporation
6 East 43rd Street, New York, NY 10017, USA
Sir Isaac Pitman (Canada) Ltd
495 Wellington Street West, Toronto 135, Canada
The Copp Clark Publishing Company
517 Wellington Street West, Toronto 135, Canada

©

H. L. Elvin
1965

ISBN 0 273 00226 0

Printed in Great Britain by Alden & Mowbray Ltd
at the Alden Press, Oxford
G3(G398:15)

PREFACE

I WISH warmly to thank Dr. W. D. Wall, Professor R. S. Peters, Professor Philip Vernon, Mrs. Jean Floud, and my wife and son for reading parts of this book when it was in draft and for making criticisms from which I have benefited greatly. It would be pleasant to say that as a result of our discussions I could now quote them as in agreement with every word that follows. But that would not be true. What I can say is that this work by a general educationist is likely to be a little less unsatisfactory to the specialists in different parts of the field than it otherwise would have been. For that help I am most grateful, even though on occasion I have not quite accommodated myself to their criticisms.

In parts I have drawn on articles that have appeared in the *Educational Review* (University of Birmingham Department of Education) and *Aspects of Education* (University of Hull Institute of Education), and I am grateful to the Editors of these publications for allowing me to make this use of them.

Lastly, a word about the title. Being an Englishman, I have written of education and contemporary English society. But let me assure any non-English reader that I do not suppose English contemporary society to be the only one of interest. I trust he will understand that I have written from within my own social context and will be content to conduct for himself any exercise in comparative education that may, therefore, be necessary.

H. L. E.

October, 1964

CONTENTS

I

THE TANGLE OF SOCIAL AND EDUCATIONAL THINKING

This book is an attempt to clarify thinking about education in its relation to the society we live in, written in the belief that unless we do this we shall have neither the education nor the society we want.

There is a prevalent notion that the theoretical discussion of education is an even greater waste of time than theoretical discussion usually is. And this is very odd, for there are few human activities in which the ideas that people hold so immediately govern what they do. When things seem to be going wrong in the education of young people some theory or theorist is commonly blamed. "How long is it," I heard a parent ask at a protest meeting about the schools in a country town, "that school has been a place where children play and home a place where harassed parents have to teach them how to work?" It was the "new methods" in education, and the theories behind them, that the parents suspected were at the root of the unsatisfactory education (as they saw it) that their children were getting at the local schools. That this suspicion was based on a good deal of misconception became clear as the meeting went on, but the point is that it was a theory that the parents blamed.

This fastening on a supposedly pernicious theory has been even more evident in the United States. John Dewey has been blamed for the shortcomings of American education and especially for its alleged lack of solid intellectual effort. His

name more than any other is linked with "progressive education," and no doubt fairly enough, though for years he
declined to associate himself with the Progressive Education
Association and when he did agree to become its honorary
President spent some effort in correcting what he felt to be its
extravagances.[1]

Dewey, however, said a very wise thing about these theoretical disputes in education. He said:[2] "Profound differences
in theory are never gratuitous or invented. They grow out of
conflicting elements in a genuine problem—a problem which
is genuine because the elements, taken as they stand, are conflicting." If this was true of educational discussion in the United
States more than half a century ago it is even more applicable
now, and the world over. We have immensely difficult
educational problems at this stage of our history, problems of
the extension of education to those who have had too little,
problems of the quality of education, problems of the relationship between education and rapidly changing societies. There
are conflicting elements in all these, and unless action is
preceded and accompanied by some sort of analysis of these
elements, and by an attempt to resolve them, action is not
likely to be very wise.

This, then, by way of justification for the present book.
But what do we mean when we speak of a theory in education?
That we do not use the word "theory" as just the opposite of
"practice" is clear from the two illustrations of its use I have
already given. Nor do we use it in the sense in which it is
used in the sciences, as a series of connected statements that
subsume our experience of some aspect of the physical world
to express our understanding of it, and that are subject to
verification by empirical tests. This is brought out in a

[1] *Dewey on Education*, ed. by M. S. DWORKIN (Teachers College, Columbia),
editor's note, p. 113.

[2] *The Child and the Curriculum* (Chicago, 1902), opening sentence.

paper[1] by Mr. Paul Hirst in which he criticizes Professor O'Connor for saying[2] that the word "theory" as used in educational contexts is generally a courtesy title, a conclusion to which the latter had come through assuming that theory in education must conform to a scientific paradigm or not be theory at all. As Hirst says, theories of science and theories of practical activities are radically different in character because they are constructed to do different things. Theories in science are "the objects, the end products of scientific investigation, they are the conclusion of the pursuit of knowledge." (I would add that this is so, in logic, even though a scientific theory may be a hypothesis arrived at by an act of intuition and confirmed only by subsequent empirical investigation.) Mr. Hirst continues: "Where, however, a practical activity like education is concerned, the place of the theory is totally different. It is not the end product of the pursuit, but rather is constructed to determine and guide the activity." Practical theories differ considerably among themselves because of the different kinds of practical activity with which they are concerned. "In some cases, as for instance in engineering, the theory is largely a reorganization of scientific theory. In the case of medicine, other elements including certain moral values are involved. Education being the kind of activity it is, the theory must range right across and draw from many kinds of knowledge, value judgements and beliefs including the metaphysical, the epistemological and the religious. All these must contribute to the peculiar character of the theory." In one part of his book O'Connor seems to be nearer to approving the kind of intellectual activity advocated by Hirst than the latter allows. He says that the critical philosopher may construct theories which tend to be interpretations of experience "in terms of

[1] Philosophy and Educational Theory (*British Journal of Educational Studies*, November, 1963).
[2] *An Introduction to the Philosophy of Education* (1957).

experience" and not, like those of metaphysicians, in terms of entities transcending experience. This, one might add, is not science either. It seems not very distant from what Mr. Hirst pictures as going on when an educationist theorizes. The chief difference between these two writers seems to be as to whether the results can be called "theories." Let us say that at least they are both "theoretical," for they are assuredly concerned with general principles emanating from and continuously related to experience.

In engaging in theoretical discussion of education, then, we are not simply resuming our knowledge in a co-ordinating formula or generalization. We are examining our practice in the light of concepts derived from a number of different disciplines, and our concern is with improvement of our practice through a more rational understanding of what we are doing. This involves, in the first place, an examination of the terms—sometimes, one must confess, the mere slogans— that we use. This activity may be at a simple linguistic or logical level; at its most discriminating it is philosophical. It also involves a survey of all relevant information. This at one level may seem to be simply descriptive, at a more sophisticated level it may be refined description through the powerful instrument of statistics, or it may be classified description in the manner of the sciences. But thirdly it involves, and properly involves, value judgements; and this (as I shall argue later) at two different levels. We can note what a society's or an individual's value judgements are, endeavouring to keep our own description value-free. Or we may enter into a discussion of the relative priority to give to different values that we or our society respect, and here we move away quite distinctly from the sciences, and some (though not all) would say from what is strict philosophy. In fact hardly anyone really keeps value judgements out of his theoretical discussion of education unless he is deliberately limiting himself to what is scientific. And this for a very good reason: the question with which we are above all concerned is what we *ought* to do, and although one can never arrive at a proof that this or that course of action is the right one because it embodies the most important values, yet discussion can assist understanding of what our purposes are and of the policies and methods most likely to achieve them.

To drive this home (for if the reader does not go along with me here he will see no point in going on with this book) I shall take a few examples from the kind of talk about education that we come across every day, and that has the most direct implications for our national policies, our schools, and our decisions as parents.

Here is the opening of an article in *The Times* on Education and the political parties[1]–

> The hottest political debates about education are not, strictly speaking, about education at all. They are about national investment, international competitiveness, social justice, the future requirements of industry, and, above all, class.

Let us take a closer look at this. We detect one immediate ambiguity, in the word "education." Does this refer to the education of individual children, or to national educational policy? If the writer means the former, he conceivably has a point. But to concede even this much is to be charitable. Some of the things the passage mentions—class, for instance, or the future requirements of industry—have a good deal to do with the education of individual children. But if the writer is referring to national educational policy—and this is what political parties might be supposed to be concerned with—then there is nothing wrong in their debating the things he mentions. Indeed, it would be very wrong if they did not. It is as if one said, in an article about government promotion

[1] "Turnover" article, April 29th, 1964.

of research into nuclear power, that the discussion was chiefly about policy as to government research stations and strictly speaking not about science at all. According to the way in which one is using the word, this is either true, obvious and proper, or it is very much open to question.

And what does "strictly speaking" mean? Does the writer imply that the imparting of knowledge to the young is education, and that bringing them up to be useful and acceptable members of society is not? The tendency of his statement is to suggest that asking questions about the social effects of education is not quite proper; and this is to be challenged.

There may of course be discussion as to what are the essential and what are only the instrumental purposes of education. It might be said (speaking rather of imagined situations) that to supply the economy with the educated and trained manpower it needs is only an instrumental purpose of education, for if we were affluent enough to survive without working at all we should still need to educate the young. There is a difference here between the economic and the social purposes of education. We cannot conceive of a time when it will not be necessary to educate the human young so that they grow up properly into human society. Some writers indeed have said that this is *the* purpose of education. There is no doubt that it is at least one essential purpose. If that is so, the question of "class" is not to be dismissed as an improper one. The kind of social person you are educating, a boy or girl to be, is indeed an educational question however strictly you are speaking.

If the writer of this passage has in mind national educational policy then it is obvious that this has to be considered in relation to many other sides of national life: because it is competing with them for funds, or because it has a bearing on their effectiveness, or because they have a bearing on its effectiveness. All of the matters he mentions are proper to consideration of national educational policy. If, however, he is talking of the education of individual children, then some of the things he mentions are not strictly part of it, while others are.

This was an actual quotation. Now let us consider three statements that are imaginary but the like of which we have all heard.

Here is the first: "People who want comprehensive schools want them for social, not for educational reasons."

And the second: "We aren't snobbish, you know, but we do want Elizabeth and Robin to speak nicely and to have good manners; and that is why we send them to a private school."

And the third: "Yes, it is unfortunate that the Public schools only take in boys from the wealthier homes, but they do give a good education and they turn out a fine type of boy, and you can't really forbid parents to make sacrifices so that their children can have such advantages."

Our first impulse when we hear statements like these is to say that they are right or wrong. But when we think about them we realize that they cannot be dismissed so simply. There may be something of both right and wrong in them. And more than one of them may be heard, in some form or other, from the same person, and one therefore has to ask if he is consistent or is on the contrary just using different assumptions according to which happen to be convenient at the moment.

Suppose, for instance, that you accept the first statement. You have made the assumption that the social education given by a school through its position in a hierarchy of schools is not proper to a consideration of its merits. There is, as we shall see, another kind of social education given by a school, its training in social habits within its own community on the assumption that these will be transferred and become character traits for life. But the experience of being in a school felt by outside society and by itself to have a certain place in a hierarchy undoubtedly has an educational effect. There are differences here among various school experiences, those of a famous independent school, of a grammar school, of a second-ary modern school, and of a comprehensive school. Although individual schools differ there are these broad differences of kind. That this is so would have to be admitted by parents who choose to send their sons to famous independent schools. One of the things they want their sons to experience is this sense of standing, and the defenders of these schools say, with a large measure of justice, that they try to give this in a way that does not simply convey a sense of privilege but of a privilege earned by discharge of duties. These parents would not only agree that this is one of the things they want for their sons from these schools but would often argue that in the long run it is much more important educationally than any book-learning they may get there. It surely follows that those who defend the independent schools in this way should be very careful of using this particular argument, that social reasons are separate from educational reasons for choosing a school. Yet those who may commonly be heard using this argument against the movement for the comprehensive school are in fact very often the same people who on another occa-sion will give social reasons for sending their own children to independent schools.

Not, of course, that our rejoinder would be enough to dismiss an attack on the comprehensive school. You may say that in a democratic society where men are going to treat each other as social equals it is reasonable to prepare the young for this in a common school; but you will have to examine the possibility that this may be inimical to some of the other pur-poses of education.

There are two fears about the comprehensive school that have to be seriously considered. One is its usual size. There are bound to be some children coming on from the primary school (quite possibly a small one) who are not very secure in their feelings, perhaps because of a difficult home background, perhaps because of temperamental qualities that give them greater need of encouragement in friendly surroundings than the average boy or girl. They can be lost if thrown suddenly into a large school, to which moreover they may have to travel daily. This is of course merely a healthy challenge to the boy or girl who is able to take it. But it is not so to all at the still tender age of eleven. In any case, all boys and girls of that age need to be known as persons by some one in the school they go to.

There are of course answers to this. One answer that may be given if there is mere debating between those who defend the comprehensive school and those who defend the Public school is that in this matter they are alike. The experience of the unhappy boy in the big rough world of the Public school is classical; in a boarding school there is no escape. The contrast to be made is between the smaller secondary school that is normal in a selective structure and the big school. The answer given by the defenders of the comprehensive school is that size is not a danger if one recognizes it, thinks about it and deals with it. In fact one can so plan a comprehensive school that though it is large in total nevertheless there are organized groupings within it such that every child can have a group of the right size for ease of accommodation to his fellows. Some comprehensive schools are now built— built physically—to provide for "houses" that are small working groups within the school, not merely conceptual groupings for competitive games and the like but real communities within the community, with their own dining rooms for instance.

Such arrangements are sensible and will almost certainly do all that is needed for the average boy and girl. But there will always be some for whom there ought to be an escape route, into a smaller more family-like school community in which they can gather confidence for a little longer before they plunge into the larger schools. People are commonly just for or against the existence of a private sector in our educational arrangements in this country. It might be sensible to ask, assuming that in principle one is against the existence of a private sector, whether there are any functions that the private sector now serves that are not served by our public sector and that will have to be accepted by it if the private sector should disappear. If that should happen, and if moreover the publicly maintained secondary schools should be on the comprehensive plan, I am sure that the public system would have to provide these escape routes into smaller school societies which are now there privately for those who can afford them or for those for whom a public educational authority will pay. The frightening truth is that our schools, which exist among other things for bridging the gap between the family and the larger community of the outside world, may actually make maladjusted citizens if as societies they are ill-adapted to the children who go into them.

This leads us to reflect that, apart from impressions, we know rather little about schools as communities. We probably know far more about some African tribes. What should we find if we set out to study how schools do function as societies, what their effective social structure and organization are, what are the sanctions that really operate within them, what the degree of tolerance to the unadjusted or the deliberately nonconformist? Some sociologists are becoming increasingly interested in what they call the "sociology of the school," that is to say the systematic study of schools of different kinds as societies in themselves.

We know more, but only a little more, about the ways in which different kinds of secondary school structure may promote or hinder intellectual development. This is important in considering the second great fear about the comprehensive school, that it may hinder the intellectual development of the ablest young people by subduing them to a school *milieu* of mediocrity. There is rather little tested evidence about this in this country. There is some from Sweden, where the new school reforms provide for a single school up to the age of fifteen or sixteen. This evidence suggests that the fairly able gain more by the stimulus of contact in the same school with the top twenty-five per cent than they lose by discouragement, and that there is no educational advantage in separate grouping for pupils of average or less than average capacity. But what of the top twenty-five per cent? The provisional evidence from Sweden suggests that up to the age at any rate of thirteen or fourteen (and the study is continuing) they are not perceptibly held back. If they were held back a little, but not much, the advocates of the school reform in Sweden would undoubtedly say that what they gain in social education through membership of a common school outweighs the little they might lose, at this stage only, in intellectual advancement. But the children who did gain most from separate teaching were the abler working-class boys; they got from it compensation in atmosphere for what many of their homes could not give.[1]

Here, clearly, we come to a difficult kind of choice, one that involves our "values." If, to take a rather extreme hypothesis, research in this country were to show that the comprehensive schools could not develop sixth-form work within range of that of the grammar schools, and therefore did militate against the intellectual advancement of the abler pupils, we should have to make a choice between things of different orders. Which should we prefer: a society in which people of different degrees of academic ability felt themselves strongly to be members of the same community, or a society in which this feeling was weaker but in which the abler boys and girls had been given special opportunities to develop their own talents

[1] A convenient summary is given by PROFESSOR HUSÉN and DR. SVENSSON in *The School Review* (Chicago, Spring, 1960).

and, quite possibly, to use them to society's advantage as well as to their own? This would be a question not of scientific research, but of values, of which of two kinds of society we wanted because we valued what it could give us more highly than the other.

In this I have of course greatly over-simplified. There would be many things we should have to take into account in any real situation. For instance, some societies are more open than others. There is more than one way to the top, whatever the particular top may be, political office, academic distinction, or what you will. There is more social mobility. Individuals are more likely to do a number of different things in the course of their working lives. There are more ways back if you have been moved away from a given line of development and wish to return to it later. In these respects American society is undoubtedly still more open than that of western European countries. The Communist countries are the most closed societies of all, for although a party functionary may be given different assignments from time to time and although an occasional figure of distinction in the arts or science may be allowed a measure of independence, by and large there is only one way to the top, through the Communist Party. In the United States the fact that you are at an educational institution without high prestige does not carry with it the danger of final placement in a hierarchy, and therefore of attendant disappointment and low morale, that assignment to a lower grade institution may have in a European country. Californian society has accepted the "Master Plan" for higher education, which certainly establishes a hierarchy as among the junior college, the state college and the University of California; but no placement is final in society. English opinion increasingly refuses to accept allocation of children to a grammar school, a technical school, or a secondary modern school; the effect is likely to last through life.

One must look in the same way at the surrounding *milieu* if one wishes to evaluate the intellectual effects of selecting or not selecting for different types of secondary school. One would need to know how strongly established the academic values were in surrounding society before one could make a judgement. American critics of American high-school education have complained very frequently in recent years that the method of the average high school is so anti-intellectual that the abler and especially the more bookish children have too little chance to develop. If it was more important years ago that the "Bearcats," the local high-school football team in "Middletown," should win their games than that the school should have a distinguished academic reputation, this is still uncomfortably near the truth for many high schools today.[1] I myself have heard a serious academic American argue that it is reasonable that the football coach of a university should be paid more than the President. Now in Sweden, where they are also establishing the comprehensive secondary school up to the age of fifteen or sixteen, the danger will certainly be less that the academic boy or girl will be swamped in a surrounding anti-intellectualism. This is simply because in Sweden parents and the public think much more of school and university as primarily academic institutions and want their children to be academically successful in them. They are more likely to be able to insist on the democratic value of a common school without risk to the abler academic children than the Americans are, except in those American communities where there is also an insistence that the high schools should put academic standards first. One does, therefore, have to look at a number of things outside the school before one can make the value-choice to which I have referred, and particularly at the general values of a society.

What kinds of question would one ask? One would ask

[1] HELEN and ROBERT LYND, *Middletown in Transition* (1937).

whether the presumed slight holding back of the more academic young people in a comprehensive school system would be likely to have permanent or only temporary effects, whether the presumed antidemocratic effects of selection for different kinds of school or institution of higher education would equally be temporary or permanent, whether the age at which selection was made was like to prove too early or not, what degree of application of the comprehensive principle we might have in mind in a mixed system, and so on. There would still in the end be a choice to make. But it could only be made with practical wisdom if full account was taken of all the social and educational circumstances. These are bound to differ from case to case

Now let us look at the second of our imaginary quotations, for it brings out another sense of the word social in relation to schooling: "We aren't snobbish, you know, but we do want Elizabeth and Robin to speak nicely and to have good manners; and that is why we send them to a private school." This is presumably some genteel suburban mother speaking, and our first impulse is to dismiss her with the curt word, "Snob!", in spite of her disclaimer.

Well, the defender of the comprehensive school who thinks that the social role of such a school is a perfectly proper one to consider, might note that this Mrs. Smith-James of 5 Acacia Avenue also appears to be invoking social considerations. So let us be sure of the ground of criticism. Are we saying that to speak properly and have good manners do not matter, or at least are of no concern for a school, or for a parent in choosing a school? Or are we saying that the notions of good speech and good manners are superficial and silly? Or would we allow that these things are important and that at this particular private school her children might in this respect be better educated, but that because it was that kind of a school they would miss more important things, social or academic? These are not idle questions. Very many parents who wish to do well by their children—even if they do dwell in suburbia—try to answer them honestly.

We could soon get into deep waters here, particularly on the question of speech, and of speech in England. Speech in this country is a social symbol, and at the same time command of the language (and this means something far beyond the usefulness of a large vocabulary and acceptable language conventions) is an immensely important factor in the structuring of an effective intelligence. The two are inextricably mixed.[1] Let us assume that we do want our children to learn to speak well, and let us assume (without going very deeply into the matter) that by "well" we mean effectively in relation to the work, the thinking and the social intercourse they will be involved in, and in a manner that will enable them to be understood without difficulty or distaste in any circles in which they may wish to move. Let us say similarly that we do want our children to be well-mannered, and not go too deeply here into what good manners are except to say that we mean ways of behaving that show consideration for other people and an understanding that you do not shock people by offending against a convention unless you have good reason to do so. Are these things important? Should we say that we prefer children to speak badly and have bad manners?

Surely not. Those who express dislike of Mrs. Smith-James's attitude will find that they are driven back to social reasons themselves. The case against her will almost certainly be, not that her arguments are social ones, but that they are the wrong sort of social arguments, that she has got her values wrong, supposing a genteel suburban speech to be necessarily the same thing as good speech, supposing suburban party

---

[1] Dr. Basil Bernstein is currently engaged in researches into this question in relation to social background. See *Journal of Child Psychology and Psychiatry*, I, p. 313, 1961; and *American Anthropology*, December, 1964.

manners (with probably different real manners in the play-
ground or out of sight and hearing) to be identical with good
manners, and in any case putting the signs of a certain social
exclusiveness above more important things, like learning to
get on with all sorts and conditions of people and rubbing
shoulders with everybody. But this has to be argued, and in
terms of the particular case. My point is that the argument will
be social *and* educational. Mrs. Smith-James may or may not
turn out to be a snob when we have looked honestly at her
case.

The third of my imaginary questions raises yet other
questions. The speaker said: "Yes, it is unfortunate that the
Public schools only take in boys from the wealthier homes,
but they do give a good education and they turn out a fine
type of boy, and you can't really forbid parents to make
sacrifices so that their children can have such advantages."
This has a slightly odd collocation of references to homes that
are wealthier than the average and that yet make sacrifices
for their children's education, it admits that the Public schools
offer a privileged start in life but plays this down with a note
of regret that they are so exclusive, and it says that they do
offer solid advantages in education and in character training,
and that you can't expect parents not to want these for their
boys. What sort of considerations must we look at here?

Let us look at the first point first. It is not so paradoxical as
might appear and it is of some importance. There is no doubt
of course that the Public schools do draw their boys from the
wealthier families. Even though a very few boys get there on
local authority grants from the local authority schools and
even though some very modestly paid professional fathers have
sons who get scholarships (for which, of course, they need
to have entered the private sector through a preparatory school
anyway), this is true enough. But it is also true that, admitting
the broad category of these families to be better off than the

average, the cost of sending perhaps two or three children to such schools is such that a considerable number of parents do have to forego other things that they might reasonably expect to enjoy, even sometimes a car, and certainly holidays abroad. They do this, first because they are responsible parents; and secondly because they think it will be worth it for their sons either in putting them in a privileged general group in later social life (and for this, even though it may not be decisive, there is much evidence—enough for parents to act on), or in giving them a better education than they might get in the local authority school (and for this there is also often a strong case to be made). There is no doubt that a good number of parents do make responsible and felt sacrifices for these advantages to their children. But when they plead this they should in all honesty remember that there are vastly more families for whom it is not possible even to contemplate making sacrifices: they are out of it altogether.

This leads us to the question of what a society ought to do about such rights of parents when the right is exercised to confer a privilege which the majority cannot enjoy and which results in enhanced inequality between citizens of the same supposedly democratic society. This unresolved conflict between the rights of parents and the rights of society has been carried into high places. You will find it in the educational clauses of the Universal Declaration of Human Rights of 1947, and you will find it in our own Education Act of 1944. It has already led to court cases in this country. As Professor Peters and others have said, the difficulty about rights is less in getting people to agree as to what are rights than in achieving a reconciliation when two or more rights, each with its own validity, clearly conflict.

The only sensible starting point is to agree that no right is, or can be considered to be, absolute. Some, it is true, might be considered to be universal. But this is not the same thing as to say that a right is absolute. The right to freedom of speech, or to freedom of religion, may be said to be universal: that is to say, they should apply to everybody and not to one person or group more than to another. But all rights are contingent, on circumstances and on each other. Freedom of speech, for instance, must be contingent on the right of others to be protected from slander. Freedom of religion cannot reasonably be held to extend to all tenets, for instance in the case of the Doukhobours who are said to be commanded by their religion from time to time to run around without any clothes on, even in Canada in the cold of winter. In this country the recent rigours of the Exclusive Brethren have raised sharp questions because of their effects on others.

We must admit that the feeling that parents have a right to do the best they can for their children is widely and strongly held. We can go further and agree at once that it is indeed in the general interests of society that parents should feel so responsible about their children. But how far should we be willing to go in backing these principles against others that may need to be taken into account? Do members of certain sects have a right to refuse to call in a doctor when their children are ill? Has society no responsibility for the rights of the children? And if the disease is infectious has it no responsibility to the right of other people to be protected from the infection? There can indeed be hard cases here. A wise society will carry tolerance to the limit. But there are limits. Most of us would be very sympathetic to a mother who had children who were starving and who stole food to give them. We should try, through society, to do something about it. But I think we should not condone the theft.

When it comes to actions that do not so much save children from intolerable privations but confer on them marked differential privileges society must clearly set limits. We want first to ascertain how far the privileges conferred are at the expense of others. There are some advantages that are in the course of nature, and some that are in the course of society, quite inevitably. We cannot help the fact that some children are potentially cleverer than others; we can only do all we can for the others. We cannot help the fact that some homes do give children a better start in life than others, not because of material and cultural advantages, but because the parents are more affectionate and more responsible. Here there is a good deal that society can do to give help to young people who do not come from such homes. Whether it can altogether make up, however, is rather doubtful.

When it comes to institutionalized privilege, and when this can be purchased, we are in a different area. This is not just a matter of envy, of saying that since so good an education cannot be enjoyed by everybody nobody shall have it. It can sometimes be argued that a privilege for a few is in the general interest of society. It is reasonable, for example, to allow a doctor to park his car outside his own house in a street in which other residents are not allowed to do so, or to give an ambulance or a fire engine right of way through the traffic. But that kind of case would be hard to establish in defence of the Public schools. A privilege is by definition an advantage, legally conferred or legally permissible, enjoyed by a person or group of persons and that other persons or groups of persons do not enjoy. This particular privilege is undoubtedly to some extent at their expense, in school and in after life. It is not candid to deny that what parents seek, and get, from sending their sons to such schools is not merely an education that is thought to be good, but a positive differential advantage. Without condemning them for doing what "every parent would do," society is entitled to ask whether it should allow it.

The argument is sometimes heard that there are so few really good schools that it would be a pity to close any of them, even if they are private. This argument naturally appeals very much to an educationist. But it won't quite do. If these independent schools are defended because they are good teaching schools, and at the same time it is admitted that the social privilege with which they are identified is wrong, then the conclusion must be, not simply that they should remain, but that action must be taken to end their social exclusiveness and at the same time retain their educational virtues. If we got to this point we should still find we had an involved discussion ahead of us, for the reason that the educational effect of a school cannot be thought of simply in terms of its teaching, and there would be some social and some educational features of each of these schools that some people would defend and others attack. But we should have reached a starting point for discussion. That we have not done so seems to me due largely to two things: the failure of the spokesmen for the Public schools to understand what the social case against them now is, and the failure of their critics to understand that there are more ways than one of bringing private institutions within the general social orbit. I should like to say something on each of these points in turn.

The simple two-nation structure of English society of the Victorian period has been very greatly modified and the concept of class (if we retain it instead of talking about "status groups") needs careful explanation and definition if it is not to distort the facts. There is much force in the point made by Mr. Crosland[1] that the distinguishing mark of social class is now "style of life." In this situation we have a division in education, into a public and a private sector, which is much sharper than anything now left in society at large, and it is a function of the independent schools not only to impress on their young a distinctive style of life but to impress on them the consciousness that to show this style of life is most import-

[1] C. A. R. CROSLAND, *The Future of Socialism*, pp. 173–8 (Cape, 1956).

ant. The question is not whether the particular style of life is good or bad—one can go on endlessly arguing whether "leadership," "responsibility," and the rest of the supposed qualities of the composite Public school boy are there in the way they are said to be and are good in the way they are developed. That doesn't get one very far. The question to examine is the social effect of taking a section of the next generation and giving it so distinctive a style of life that, in spite of many later modifying forces, the beneficiaries feel they have something very much like membership of a socially superior club.

Reformers among the defenders of the Public school are commonly ready to take in more boys from the publicly maintained schools, as the Fleming Committee recommended twenty years ago. But nobody has ever been very happy about this kind of solution. The reason is clear from the remark of the Headmaster of Eton when the Report came out. He said that they would not mind at all taking boys in from the public elementary schools—but on one condition, that these boys conformed to Eton and did not expect Eton to conform to them. If one considers three recent, and very different, books about these schools one finds evidence on the same point. Mr. John Wilson, in his *Public Schools and Private Practice*,[1] calls a good deal of bluff and is very amusing on, for instance, the public relations side of these schools; but in the end he is for them. Mr. Rupert Wilkinson in his book *The Prefects*[2] says that he does not enter into moral judgements and is concerned only to study whether a particular method for training leaders in society now works. In fact he comes much nearer to an imaginative understanding of the role of these schools in society than most writers on the subject. Mr. John Dancy, of Marlborough, in his *The Public Schools and the*

[1] Allen and Unwin, 1962.
[2] Oxford, 1962.

Future,[1] has written a very sober and fair-minded book. He had access to Mr. Wilkinson's book in its earlier form as a doctoral thesis and he finds it basically just in its assessment of the Public school type for, say, the period 1900–40. But he argues that there have been real modifications since then. For instance, one hears now of "responsibility" rather than "leadership" (the cynic might say that was neat public relations work). Moreover the type of man produced is what industry, for instance, wants, whether it ought to or not. Somehow one feels that this is all good, temperate arguing; but that it does not get to the heart of the matter.

This is not whether, in a democracy, we should all have the same style of life—speak alike, look alike, dress alike, have the same tastes and preferences, and so on. Life would be dull if we did. The two important questions are: first, whether it is on the whole true to say that there is broadly a style of life inculcated by the independent schools which does seriously mark their members off from the rest of us; and second, whether with the present developments of our society in mind this is on balance a good thing or a bad. If we came to the conclusion that there was such a socially divisive effect, and that it was out of accord with the way in which we want our society to go, then a third question would arise: assuming that in the style of life itself there are some qualities we respect and like, though others we may not, can the former be reasonably encouraged in a more unified education system without the special exclusive cultivation they now get in the independent boarding schools?

It is very difficult to explain to an insider what one means (if one is an outsider) about this "style of life."[2] Yet the outsiders are very conscious of it. If they try to explain what they

[1] Faber, 1963.

[2] For an amusing account of the symbols of this see Mr. John Vaizey's account in *The Establishment* (Blond, 1959).

feel there are always two replies. The first is: "But we really aren't snobbish—that just isn't a fair statement any more." One can only comment that in a sense this is often true: but there is an air that leadership (responsible leadership, of course) is a prerogative. And the grammar-school boy and the technical-college boy are feeling increasingly, in virtue of what? The second reply—and this is true enough too—is that in the publicly maintained system there are also gradations of social prestige and of assumed superiority according to the kind of school one has been to. The only real answer to this is to admit it, to say (fairly) that it is not on the whole so socially divisive as the major cleavage between the public sector as a whole and the private sector as a whole, and to do something about this as well. What is needed is social imagination, to understand the questions that must be put about the independent schools given the modifications that have taken place since the war and that are continuing in English society as a whole.[1]

Now let us turn to the other side, where there is a similar lack of imagination. As our supposed speaker said, the best of these schools are very good teaching schools. Maybe they should be, with their favourable ratio of staff to boys, their

[1] I must here confess that I found the choice of photograph for the dust cover of this book irresistible, but it was in fact taken before the last war. I am told that young Etonians do not now have to wear this strange garb on the occasion of the cricket match with Harrow at Lord's, but I find this, I admit, a comment of minor social significance. The significant change is another one. To the "urchins" in the picture the young Etonians are not objects of resentment, but of wonder: they come from another world. The sons of the "urchins" now look a little different too; they may be in grammar schools or even perhaps at Oxford or Cambridge in one or two instances. But because social changes have brought the two groups a little nearer to one another the differences in style of life, though modified, are likely to be felt as more, not as less, of an anachronism. As the head boy of the L.C.C. boarding school, Woolverstone Hall, said rudely but pointedly to a B.B.C. questioner who asked how they felt in their matches against the Public schools: "What's special about Public school boys? They've only got more of the loot."

superior endowment of playing fields, and other advantages. But it is not unreasonable to connect this teaching excellence with the considerable degree of freedom given to the head-masters, above all in the planning of studies and in the selection of staff. There is a better case for nourishing academic excellence than social exclusiveness. Can the one be retained without the other? The answer surely turns on our ability to relate social aims with administrative arrangements.

R. H. Tawney used to say that it was of no use thinking that you could deal with the social problems raised by the independent schools without tackling their Governing Bodies, and above all getting rid of the preponderance of retired generals and bishops on them. Of course they would stand for the Establishment while that was so. But Tawney also said there was no need to suppose that, therefore, you must put Eton under the Buckinghamshire County Council. What *via media* might there be? It is odd that the Labour Party has traditionally resented the principle of the Direct Grant schools, for here surely is the key to an answer. No doubt some of these schools minister to a sense of social exclusiveness in the minds of some parents, but the best of them show that schools largely within the public orbit can challenge the independent schools successfully on the academic ground. Some of their headmasters and headmistresses would be quite content to have all their places open to merit alone, so long as they were left with the degree of freedom to run their own schools which they now enjoy and that on the whole they have well justified. But how could this be reconciled with the increasing acceptance of the comprehensive principle? As I shall try to show later, this is by no means an insoluble problem if we can bring some reasonable administrative imagination to bear on our secondary-school organization. It is possible, without breaking too catastrophically with the past, to reorganize both the private and the public sectors so that they can gradually merge together. At the moment, however, I am only drawing attention to the prerequisites for a solution: social imagination on the part of the defenders of the independent schools, administrative imagination on the part of those who want to bring them into the public orbit. More basically the problem is bound to be intractable unless we first think out the principles of reconciliation between rights and values, social and educational, that are in apparent conflict.

I hope that with these four illustrations, one actual and three (in form at least) imaginary, I have persuaded the reader that discussion of the theory of education, in social and educational terms equally, is of the greatest practical importance. After this brief look at the subject he may agree that a better analysis of the terms we use and of the assumptions we make, a greater attempt to be consistent, and above all a clearer understanding of the values we stand for, would be of practical use. For this kind of discussion we really need a new term. On the analogy of socio-economic one could say "socio-educational" but that is rather horrible, so I shall continue to use the phrase "thinking about education and society," making clear that I mean one, not two separate, kinds of thinking.

In the next chapter I shall ask where we may look, in existing disciplines, for the groundwork of our thinking about this subject.

PART I · STUDIES

In any realm of human conduct the most important question
we have to ask is: what we *ought* to do. We must know the
facts of a situation, its history, and the direction in which
things are moving. If it is in an area of life in which human
beings have long had to act and presumably always will have
to act, we need to know what the relevant sciences have to
say and, equally, what the moralists and philosophers have
thought to be more and less important. We have to think
about our own general attitude to the kind of problem
involved. Then we have to make decisions and to act upon
them. This is as true in education as in anything else. As parents
we may want all the knowledge and information we can get,
and we shall probably listen to a good deal of advice. We
have already our own general attitudes to the bringing up of
children and to schools and universities. But the question we
must ask, and try to answer, is: what ought we to do about
our children's education? It is the same in national educational
policy. Sooner or later we have to decide: decide what scale of
educational provision we want, decide what kind of educational arrangements will conduce to the benefit of the country,
decide what social arrangements will most assist education.
We have to develop a general attitude for the purposes of
continuing general policy, and in endless particular matters we
have collectively to decide what we ought to do.

Educational problems are always complex and, as we have
seen already, all the good arguments will not be on one side.
The scientists and the philosophers can help, but they cannot
give particular practical answers. We need the data of the

scientists. The philosophers should help us to get our concepts clearer, and they may (if they think this proper to philosophy) initiate discussion as to the relative value of different things. But if scientists use the word "ought" at that moment they cease to be scientific. The philosophers love discussing "ought" but they are quite clear that you cannot make a straight deduction from a philosophical statement to give you an answer to a practical problem.

Nevertheless the relevant studies are indispensable. If a society or its individual members do not understand what these studies have to say about education and society they will not make good decisions. With such understanding they will still have to make the decisions themselves, and they may well not all be of one mind; but they should make wiser decisions. So in this chapter I shall by implication be demonstrating three things. First that the necessary preliminary to answering any "ought" questions about education and society is sound factual knowledge, organized scientifically. Second, that scientific techniques are only one kind of technique of discussion we must use, because for our purpose they are in themselves incomplete. And thirdly, that even though discussions of "ought" questions cannot give us decisive answers on which we shall all agree they can assist us to make better decisions.

I shall consider in turn the academic disciplines that are relevant to the study of education and society. These are especially sociology, psychology, social philosophy, and comparative education (and all, I should add, should be studied in the light of history). But in regard to the first three I shall escape from doubtful nouns to easier adjectives. I shall talk of sociological, psychological, and philosophical determinants of our thinking rather than of the contribution of sociology, psychology, and philosophy to it. This is because I do not want to get involved in arguments as to whether this or that statement is, for instance, "sociology," sociology being claimed as a science and some of the things that sociologists write in their books being clearly non-scientific (and not necessarily the worse for that). Similarly, with the psychologists. As to philosophy, who knows, now, what is philosophy? If you do as so many philosophers have done and indicate the kind of society we ought to have, that now is likely to be held to be not philosophy. So be it. I recognize the case that can be made, and up to a point welcome it. If we cannot be absolutely sure that the assistance given us is in the strictest sense sociology or psychology or philosophy, at least we can speak of determinants of our thinking that are, in a general way, sociological, psychological, or philosophical. These, then, I now propose to discuss. And I shall end this part by considering the influence on our thinking of what different societies have done to fashion a relationship between education and society. Through such comparisons we may greatly improve the perspective in which we see our own problems. To begin, then, with the sociological determinants of our thinking about education and society.

II

SOCIOLOGICAL

THERE is a welcome tendency now to pay greater attention to the social setting of education. We have long understood that you cannot keep a nation healthy simply by attending patients when they are ill or watching over the health of individuals; all sorts of social and preventive measures must be taken to safeguard the health of a community. In the same way, we now realize with greater force than we did (though psychologists have made the point before) how limited is the scope of a teacher in a school in a bad neighbourhood, how handicapped children are who live in such neighbourhoods, and how all this mocks our hopes for equality in education, and for more equality through education.

Sociologists have here reinforced what social psychologists have known. As I have said, I do not want to get drawn deeply into arguments as to whether studies I refer to are or are not sociology. For instance, the Newsom Report, to which I shall refer later, is no doubt not, as such, a work of sociology, but it does adduce evidence that in a general way is sociological. And it is very relevant to our purpose.

Some sociologists have studied the relationships of education to society in a severe and incontestably scientific way (even though their choice of field of inquiry may have had strong value motivation behind it—which is legitimate enough), whereas others have joined to the objective inquiries very cogent recommendations for action which have carried value judgements with them. The great effort to introduce rigorous methods of inquiry into a field of human life where rigour can only be achieved with great effort is to be applauded, and of course what claims to be work of research objectivity must prove to be so. But the social investigator is more likely to make consequential policy judgements with force and yet with balance than the rest of us. However this may be, it is clear that the question as to what we ought to do is so insistent that even those who call themselves social scientists often address themselves to it. But we must here distinguish between two uses of the word "ought." When we express doubts as to whether a work of sociology is value-free, we imply that the writer has in his mind "ought" assumptions that he has taken for granted. Most sociologists would think it their duty to reduce this area of value assumptions as much as possible. They accept Hume's classical warning against moving by sleight-of-hand from a statement that something is to a statement that something ought to be. Even Gunnar Myrdal, who is unorthodox in that he argues that a value structure in the mind is what gives coherence and force to a social scientist's thinking, insists that the values must be brought forward and not hidden so as to deceive the reader.[1]

However, the word "ought" may also be used in a merely hypothetical or consequential sense. A writer may say, "If we want that, then we ought to do this." Strictly this should not involve a value decision, but only a sequence in logic. The difficulty of course is that behind "ought" used in this way there is often a value-tinged feeling, as if the writer were adding "and indeed we ought to." Writers in this mode of discourse are not writing works on ethical theory. They are normally concerned with policy and practice and feel themselves justified in giving themselves freedom to make recommendations, hoping that most people will share any value judgements they imply.

[1] GUNNAR MYRDAL: *Value in Social Theory* (Routledge and Kegan Paul, 1958).

Take, for example, one of the most illuminating contributions to our thinking about society and education made in recent years, Dr. J. B. Mays' *Education and the Urban Child*.[1] Dr. Mays is a Senior Lecturer in Social Science in the University of Liverpool, but his book, though I am sure impeccable in its research methods, is full of "ought" and "must" sentences. He could have written his book without them and left us to draw our own conclusions. Some would say that he would have been not only scientifically more proper, but the stronger in his policy effect if he had done so. His "must" and "ought" sentences raise a few new questions on which there might be different value judgements, and in that sense do not follow with absolute logic from his findings. Yet I am not sure. I suspect that his book had more force because he said not only "Look, this is the state of things I have found in the schools of a decaying area in Liverpool," but also, "And we must do something about it, things like the following." The study of a society is a mixed sort of study anyway. What purports to be scientific must be genuinely so. But this will take us only part of the way, and we need not necessarily object if a social investigator points out what he thinks the rest of the way should be. I should say this even if I did not altogether agree that his recommendations for the rest of the way were right: I would like to hear what he had to say.

Let us follow this up a little with the example I have referred to. Dr. Mays made his study of the schools, in relation to the neighbourhood of a decaying area of inner Liverpool. He found in this area a more or less stabilized pattern of living which in some respects conflicted with the norms of society as a whole. There was in this area what he called a sub-culture. Among its characteristics that were immediately significant for education were a higher than usual degree of truancy,

[1] University of Liverpool Press, 1962.

delinquency, and mental backwardness. But more than this; here was a way of life that was foreign to the young teacher coming into the area from a grammar school and training college or university, and the teacher's way of life was just as foreign to the children. (The most graphic demonstration that this is important may be seen with the varied success of our teachers from India or Pakistan in schools with immigrant children: such a teacher may do quite brilliantly with these children and yet find it very hard to succeed with English children because their attitudes, their relationship to each other, are not mutually accepted, so that there is no psychological basis on which to build teacher-pupil co-operation.) Dr. Mays quoted Mr. Edward Blishen on the "fundamental incomprehension" that often occurs when a young teacher meets a secondary modern class in such an environment. Somehow, says Dr. Mays, these down-town schools must make a break-through and establish a bridge-head of mutual respect and understanding. He goes on—

> This is a task which calls for immense courage, great imagination and extensive physical and financial provision. The children of exceptional merit from such areas will always have a chance to rise. The children of slightly less ability who could make use of equal opportunities should also be given the same chance to improve their lot in life. The remnant must not be written off as "children of less ability" and offered a substandard education against which they will not protest and which probably they will passively accept. Here and now the problem must be faced of bridging the gap between conflicting cultures, between the teachers and their pupils, between the grammar school and the board school traditions. The board school tradition, which is a hang-over from the day when society was much more deeply stratified and divided, must be eradicated entirely if the objective is ever to be achieved. (p. 103)

There can be few people who would not agree with what Dr. Mays says here, or would not feel that it follows from his investigations. Yet he has gone into a different kind of discourse. This is not the language of science. The passage is thick with value judgements. It is expressive of the kind of society Dr. Mays would like to see. Indeed, in the "Conclusions" with which he ends the book, Dr. Mays tells us what we ought to do about the situation he has found. He has many "must" sentences. He says that "every school must itself strive to become a true community." He says that the school must achieve a better relationship with the life of the neighbourhood. He says that the curriculum must become more vocational and that this does not necessarily mean a narrowing of ideals. Value judgements all of them, both social and educational. Should they have been left out, since sociology is supposed to be a social science?

On balance I think not. The book is more of a whole because they are there. What is the point of getting the facts if we aren't going to do something about them? Yet if value judgements are included in such books they must not prejudice the objectivity of the inquiry: that is obvious. But, also, the reader must be aware of which realm of discourse he is in at each moment. The facts he cannot question, without undertaking another inquiry. The value statements he may. For instance, there might reasonably be more than one opinion about the degree to which education in these schools ought to be vocational, and an opinion that it might well be less so than Dr. Mays desires would not necessarily conflict with his factual evidence. It would imply a different response to it. Again, the desire that these schools should have a better relationship with the life of the neighbourhood needs some analysis. "Better" cannot mean "more like," for the life of the neighbourhood has been described as very much in need of improvement, and Dr. Mays recognizes that a good school can help in improving it. Then how is the relationship to be "better?" In what ways can it become closer without losing its standards? There are of course answers, and many a good school in a slum neighbourhood has found them, but they go beyond science.

I make this point to emphasize that we are confronted by problems that do indeed invite a mixed sort of study. There must be a factual, and one may properly say a scientific, basis. And then there are bound to be reflections that involve value judgements. If we think of sociology as social science then only the first part, strictly, is sociology. If we think of it as social study, then all of it can be. Some writers prefer to keep the two distinct. Some move in both realms of discourse within the covers of a single book. This does not seem to me to matter vastly. Certainly there is no call for dogmatic rules about it. What does matter is that we should call science only that which is science, and that we should understand that if we address ourselves to "must" and "ought" questions we are moving beyond science.

With this clarification as to the different kinds of study we may be looking at I should like to ask what we can learn about the social setting of our education that should influence our thinking about education and society. No doubt one could find more or less well documented examples from many countries and from more than one period of history, but since in this country we are living now in a period of intense interest in this question let us see what light can be thrown on it by studies made here in very recent years.

It might be useful to review some of the changes in opinion about our education in the twenty years since the Act of 1944 and to consider how far sociological inquiries have contributed to these changes.

Whatever afterthoughts we may now have, there is no doubt that the 1944 Act marked a great step forward in education in this country. It established secondary education for all up to the age of fifteen and accepted in principle the raising of the age to sixteen. It did get away from the conception of education for the common people as education for the poor and asserted the right of all children to an education according to their age, aptitudes, and ability. It is not surprising that the Act was felt to be something of a charter of educational rights, as an enactment which would give far greater equality of opportunity. Even the establishment of the "tripartite" system of secondary education which followed was defended as fairer to children of different levels and kinds of ability than a simple opening of the academic secondary schools to all.

Not all of this need be unsaid. But two major footnotes would now be in nearly everybody's mind. The first is, that for reasons nearly all of which are directly social, much more inequality remains than we had supposed would; and second, that the virtually final division of children of eleven into groups going to different kinds of secondary school has proved much less possible with fairness than we had expected. These two shifts are due (apart from the pretty shrewd hunches of parents) to sociological and psychological investigations respectively. But since the psychologists have shown that social environment is a bigger factor than we had supposed in success in tests of intelligence both are largely based on examination of factors in our society.

The assumption that most people made about the 1944 Act was that if you could determine children's ability fairly (and in particular if you could determine the level of their intelligence independently of what they had been able to achieve academically up to the date of the test), and if you then gave them an equal chance to get into the kind of school appropriate to their level or type of ability, there would be something like fair treatment for all. Although psychologists had noted that social factors operated against a child from a working-class home, public opinion, when it came to selecting for the post-war tripartite system, would not have accepted a weighting designed to counterbalance this. With the equality of opportunity that it was popularly supposed the 1944 Act would bring, it was assumed that people would be able to pass with much greater freedom from one level of society to another. In 1949 a large-scale investigation was undertaken at the London School of Economics, under Professor Glass, into this question of social mobility. But the investigation soon raised the question as to what was the relationship in this country between educational opportunity and social class. There followed a study by Mrs. Floud and her collaborators Dr. Halsey and Dr. Martin, *Social Class and Educational Opportunity*, published in 1956. Mrs. Floud, in her Introduction, says that the earlier investigation had shown how unequal were the chances of a secondary education up to 1939 for boys and girls in the different classes of the population, but this investigation had not related this fact to the social distribution of intelligence or to the extent to which social factors might influence the process of selection for secondary school. The new study was an attempt to "document" the post-war educational revolution in this way. What did it reveal?

First, that taking ability *as measured by intelligence tests*, the opportunity to enter the secondary grammar schools was indeed much closer to ability than ever before. Yet marked social inequality remained. Two localities were studied in depth. In Middlesbrough one working-class boy in eight was admitted compared with nearly one in three of the sons of clerks; and in south-west Hertfordshire one in seven as compared with nearly one in two of sons of clerks. How are we to explain these differences?

Obviously, as Mrs. Floud pointed out, the question as to how far social factors influence the scores in measurements of intelligence is at once implied. Professor Vernon had already indicated in his book, *The Bearings of Recent Advances in*

Psychology on Educational Problems (1955) that the "intelligence" that was being measured was in considerable part an acquired characteristic. It was not Mrs. Floud's purpose to tackle this problem directly, but her study did investigate the degree to which social factors—the material circumstances of the home and the neighbourhood, the size of the family, the social aspirations of the parents for their children—might be correlated with entry to the grammar school. The findings made it clear that here, in social circumstances experienced before the age of eleven, were deep roots of inequality of opportunity.

Lastly, there was an inequality at the end of the compulsory period of school attendance. Who left at the first possible opportunity? Many of the ablest. For these this was not only early, but premature leaving, for they might have profited greatly by staying on. The social waste that was involved in giving insufficient education to some of our ablest boys and girls was now being pushed forward from the point of entry to the secondary school to the point of entry (or non-entry) to the sixth form.

The study of Mrs. Floud and her collaborators gave a factual and statistical basis for much more anxious thinking as to the degree to which the hopes of the immediate post-war period were being realized. But a work of greater popular impact, the Crowther Report, appeared in 1959. This was a socially based report. Not merely did its first chapters, after a descriptive opening, go into questions of demographic, social and economic change before coming on to educational matters as such, but many of its conclusions were based on social surveys of a kind now familiar enough but novel then in a government report on education. One of these surveys was of the entrants to national service as grouped by the Army in its six ability ratings. What was found stuck in the public mind: half the National Service recruits to the Army who were rated in the two top ability groups[1] had left school at fifteen.[2]

The next survey to which I would like to refer is that conducted by Dr. J. W. B. Douglas, Director of the Medical Research Unit at the London School of Economics, and published under the title *The Home and the School*.[3] This survey supplements Mrs. Floud's conclusion that the waste of ability had been pushed forward to the point of entry to the sixth form by showing how much greater it is than we realized even before the entry to the secondary school. The survey considered some 5,362 children, all born in the first week of March, 1946, and coming from every kind of family and social class all over the country. It followed them through their years in the primary schools until they had sat the "eleven plus" and had been allocated to their secondary schools. Here are some of the findings.

Take as the measure of real demand for grammar schools the proportion of parents who opt for grammar schools and who are also willing to let their children stay on till seventeen. Thirty-one per cent of the mothers did this. Fifty-nine per cent of these were disappointed in their hopes. This gives the measure of the shortage of grammar school places in terms, not of course of suitability for grammar school education, but of demand for it. Many of the mothers bitterly resented the refusal to admit their children. Only two-thirds of the children thought by their teachers to be suitable for grammar school education went there.

Secondly, how do children fare who come from different kinds of home? Homes were classified as satisfactory or not in terms of physical amenities (degree of over-crowding, independent kitchen and bathroom, and so on), and something very

[1] As revealed by a mixed battery of tests, some of which were non-verbal and perhaps not very well correlated with academic aptitude.

[2] *15 to 18*: Report of the Central Advisory Council for Education—England. Conclusions and Recommendations, no. 671, and Vol. II, part two.

[3] MacGibbon and Kee, 1964.

disturbing was learned about the effect of bad home conditions on performance in tests of composite intellectual performance. Working-class children from unsatisfactory homes become progressively handicapped; they make lower scores in the tests given at eleven than in those given at eight, losing an average of 0·66 points of score during these three years; whereas those from satisfactory homes improve their score during the same period by an average of 0·04 points.

In general there is a cumulative disadvantage for the working-class child. By the time he is eleven, says the Report, the clever manual-working-class child has fallen behind the middle-class child of similar ability at eight years, and equally the backward manual-working-class child shows less improvement than the backward middle-class child. This has its effect on chances of entering the grammar school. The difference in chance between classes is most marked. Fifty-four per cent of upper-middle-class children, but only eleven per cent of lower-manual-working-class children go to grammar schools; and not all of the poor achievement of the working-class children is explained by their lower measured ability. The other differentiating factors may lie in personal qualities (e.g. their industry or behaviour) or in the degree of encouragement they get from their parents.

Then again, primary schools differ considerably in their success in getting pupils through the "eleven plus." Schools with the best records attract pupils from the middle classes and those whose parents are anxious for them to succeed. Children at these schools draw ahead between the ages of eight and eleven in their test scores. And again "streaming" in primary schools (putting children into classes according to their supposed grade of ability) is more rigid than many people have supposed; and the manual-working-class children show a severe deterioration in performance if they are put in the lower streams. The degree to which they deteriorate *because* they are put in lower streams, rather than because of the poor earlier experience that in part put them there, remains to be decided. But this does not affect the point I am making.

In conclusion Dr. Douglas says: "The evidence set out in this book gives strong reasons for believing that much potential ability is wasted during the primary school years and mis-directed at the point of secondary selection." He is speaking with the schools in the public sector in mind. "When the criterion of selective secondary education is broadened," he adds, "to include private as well as grammar and technical schools, all semblance of social equality vanishes."

These are the findings of a careful factual and statistical inquiry.

Now let us look at the other end of the educational spec-trum. In his Introduction to Dr. Douglas's book Professor Glass made this transition, writing while the Committee on Higher Education (the "Robbins" Committee) was still discussing its draft Report. He pointed out that about twenty per cent of children have I.Q.s of 113 and over, but that, by the time the survey children had become sixteen, fifteen per cent of this highly intelligent group had already left full-time education, four-fifths of these being working-class children. More would leave before the age of entry to the university was reached. At present between four and five per cent of an age group enter the universities of this country. If the level were raised to those with an I.Q. of 120 we should still have to double that proportion. How much higher, concluded Pro-fessor Glass, our target ought to be than it actually is. Let us see what the Robbins Report, and its surveys, had to say about this.

The Robbins Report[1] was very thoroughly documented. Six major sample surveys were commissioned, other inquiries were drawn on for factual and statistical material, and the

[1] H.M.S.O., 1963.

services of the relevant government departments were readily placed at the disposal of the Committee. The results of this work may be seen in the Appendices to the Report, of which Appendix One, *The Demand for Places in Higher Education*, is the most important for our present purpose.

The very first table presents evidence that pulls one up short. It shows that the proportion of children who reach full-time higher education is about six times as great in the families of non-manual workers as in those of manual workers; the chances of reaching courses of degree level are about eight times as high. The second table shows that children with fathers in professional and managerial occupations are twenty times more likely to enter full-time higher education than are those with fathers in semi- and unskilled jobs.

"Naturally," might be the reply. "These children of professional parents are more intelligent." Well: are they? What does this really mean? If they are more intelligent is their more favourable treatment in rough proportion to this superiority, or does it seriously exceed it? The Robbins Report establishes that superior innate intelligence is certainly not the only reason why a greater proportion of middle-class children reach higher education. We have seen from Dr. Douglas's survey that unequal social conditions have been one factor in setting back working-class children at the age of eleven as compared with the age of eight. Even so, when grammar school children (says the Robbins Report) are grouped according to their measured intelligence at the age of eleven, as well as their final educational attainment, one finds that among children of a given intelligence a much higher proportion of those from middle-class homes reach higher education than of those from working-class homes. Table 4 of Appendix One shows that the proportion of children with a measured intelligence of between 115 and 129 who entered full-time higher education was thirty-four per cent for middle-class children and only fifteen per cent for those from manual-working-class homes. The difference is less striking, but still marked, for children of higher intelligence still.

We have seen that the gap between the educational chances of the working-class and the middle-class child widens progressively in the earlier school years. The Robbins Report shows that it goes on widening. This, let us repeat, is among children of the same potential, but from different social backgrounds. Taking the same group, children whose measured intelligence at eleven was between 115 and 129, a quarter more middle-class children than working-class children got at least five "O" levels, two-thirds more reached two "A" levels, and over twice as many entered full-time degree courses.

This is a sad cumulative picture for those who thought that the 1944 Act had brought equality of educational opportunity into our society. It shows that the social factors affecting education are more intractable than we formerly thought. But they are not all equally intractable. The factors suggested by Dr. Douglas for the disparities of educational opportunity in the primary school and in entry to the secondary school— homes without reasonable amenities, culturally deprived neighbourhoods, lack of parental interest and encouragement —cannot be dealt with by Education Acts alone.[1] But one disparity noted by the Robbins Report, the differences at "A" level, is much more susceptible to educational action. It arises largely, says the Report, because working-class children tend to leave school earlier. Those working-class children who do stay on—and this is encouraging—are on average as

[1] The Statistical Adviser to the Robbins Committee had available to him the results of the Douglas surveys published after the Robbins Report had appeared, and section 2 of part II of Appendix One (paras. 12 to 25) gives a useful summary of the combined Douglas-Robbins picture.

successful as their counterparts in other social groups. This suggests that there is some scope for manoeuvre for the educationist *per se*, although the real lion in the path now is the social one.

But surely, and by and large, we are doing better since the passing of the 1944 Act? The answer of the Robbins Committee investigators is yes—and no. Total provision has increased and so for a child of given ability the chance of educational success has been steadily rising, but the differentials between social classes, the *relative* chances of reaching higher education for middle-class and working-class children are much the same in the early 1960s as they were in the period 1928–47. The proportion of children getting five or more "O" levels is lower among children from working-class families who pass into grammar schools in the upper third of the eleven plus intake than among children from professional and managerial homes in the lower third of the eleven plus intake And since 1953 the proportions have risen significantly in the highest occupational group, where the "pool of ability" might have been thought to be more nearly exhausted. For school as for higher education, conclude these reporters, there has probably not been much narrowing of class differences between 1950 and 1960.[1]

Finally in this review of current studies of the social handicaps to good education we must look at some descriptions of the worst situations that exist. I have already referred to *Education and the Urban Child* by Dr. Mays. Although this

[1] The evidence collected and analysed for the Robbins Committee has led some commentators (e.g. Mrs. Floud) to say that much more radical proposals than the Committee made are necessary if we are to deal with inequality of access to higher education. I think this is true, and important. I would not, however, accept it as a criticism of the Committee, since their task began with the situation as it was to be found at the age of eighteen. This, however, is a minor qualification to the statement. The real trouble is that at eighteen the damage has already been done. The need is for an overall view and an overall policy.

does contain value-judgement statements (rightly, as I have said) it is of course primarily a study in scientific depth of the situation in one very difficult and subnormal locality. A broader treatment of the same theme is to be found in the Newsom Report on the education between the ages of thirteen and sixteen of pupils of average or less than average ability.[1] This adduces a good deal of evidence, often of an illustrative kind, that carries conviction. Forty per cent of the sample of secondary modern type schools considered by the Committee had buildings that were seriously inadequate, and in areas that the Committee felt could be described as slum areas four out of five schools were seriously inadequate in terms of buildings and elementary amenities. A new, good school building in such an area helps. But it cannot solve the educational problem by itself. In the interests of education the Committee recommended study, and action, to deal with the social problem in the slum areas.

The Committee (more strictly the Central Advisory Council for Education, since the "Committee" was simply the Council in this phase of its work) had a survey made of 150 modern schools and in particular of some 6,000 fourth-year pupils in them. One very encouraging conclusion was that the evidence, based largely on reading tests, showed that there had been a marked educational improvement comparing 1961 with 1956. A second conclusion was that the poorer showing of the special group of schools in slum areas was substantially the effect of the poorer environment.

Another finding of the Newsom Report seems to offer a more encouraging picture of the gap between the classes than the other evidence we have referred to. From 1951 to 1961 there was an improvement of about seventeen per cent in the number of boys and girls in the country getting five or more "O" level passes, but within this there was a degree

[1] *Half Our Future*, H.M.S.O., 1963.

of levelling up between the classes, the proportion of passes going to boys from the homes of unskilled and semi-skilled workers rising from thirty-one per cent to forty-one per cent, and of girls from such homes from twenty-eight per cent to thirty-four per cent. The Report says this may be regarded as a first instalment of what may be expected as manual workers become increasingly familiar with what secondary education offers to their children. One may hope that this will be so. But in its main emphasis the Newsom Report is yet one more document forcing us to think more seriously than we have about the social setting and basis of education.

If we were to sum up this review of recent contributions by social investigators what would we say? Something like a major development in thinking has taken place, and it is almost entirely due to the kind of patient, detailed work I have been describing. The change in outlook that has taken place was summed up by Mrs. Floud in a paper[1] she read at a conference called by the Organization for Economic Co-operation and Development at Kungälv in Sweden in 1961—

> Until 1945 [she said] roughly speaking, the problem of social class in education was seen, by social investigators and policy makers alike, primarily as a *barrier to opportunity*. The problem was an institutional one: how to secure equality of access for children of comparable ability, regardless of their social origins, to institutions of secondary and higher education designed for, and still used in the main by, the offspring of the superior classes. In so far as social class was seen to influence educational *performance* the problem was conceived of as a material one: how to mitigate the handicaps of poverty, malnutrition and over-crowding by using the schools as social agencies—by distributing free milk and meals to necessitous children and developing the school medical services. Only in the post-war period has the continuing attempt to democratize secondary and higher education in unfamiliar conditions of full

[1] Published in *Ability and Educational Opportunity*, ed. by A. H. HALSEY, O.E.C.D., 1961.

employment and widespread prosperity confronted us with the need to formulate the problem more subtly and to see social class as a profound influence on the *educability* of children.

This is a key new thought. Once it has been assimilated by the policy makers, national and local, modifications are bound to take place in educational and social policy. I have taken this as my example of the crucial role of social studies in our educational thinking, because it affords evidence of such an important shift in attitude, because it is a recent phenomenon still imperfectly worked out and still imperfectly understood even in principle, but of course chiefly because of its bearing on the general argument with which I am here concerned: that thinking about society, on a basis of attested knowledge, is an indispensable component of thinking about education. The fact that the example comes from the United Kingdom is merely incidental. Were we considering any other country, either where sociology is an established study or where it is not and needs to be, we should come to the same conclusion. Not least important is its bearing on our ideas of values, as Mrs. Floud plainly hints. What did we think we meant by equality of educational opportunity? The line we drew in our minds between equality of opportunity on the one hand, and equality itself on the other, will not do. To achieve the equality of opportunity, as these recent studies have revealed its meaning, we have to move much further in the direction of real equality.

There is one question we have so far left out. As soon as we use the word "educability" we move into the field of the psychologist. What is the "measured intelligence" we have been speaking of and that these reports and surveys so frequently invoke? However much we modify our notions of equality of opportunity in a liberal direction it surely remains true that not all children are "educable" to the same point. When William Godwin, who believed in the perfectibility of human nature through education, said he could even educate tigers, a doctor who remained sceptical said he would like to see him in a cage with two of his pupils. With human beings, too, there are limits beyond which sensible people will not expect education to work. As the Robbins Report says: "No one who has taught young people will be disposed to urge that it is only the difference in educational opportunity that makes the difference between a Newton or a Leonardo and Poor Tom the Fool." Then how do we measure the limits within which social action might realize different children's educability and beyond which it is only likely to be so much waste of time, effort and money? It would certainly seem as if Providence has distributed abilities in a way that shows very imperfect concern for notions of abstract equality. If we now realize that some of the apparent inequality is man-made inequality of social opportunity, it certainly is not all that. How far is it really a fact of nature? For an answer to this question we must turn to the psychologists.

III

PSYCHOLOGICAL

THERE are several kinds of psychological study that contribute to our thinking about education and society. In a fuller work than this it would be necessary to give an account of studies in at least two fields to which I shall make only passing reference in order to concentrate on the field that has greatest bearing on our immediate discussion.

If we want to come to some conclusion as to how far our children and young people could benefit from further educational provision we have to think of improvements affecting education that are social, and we have to think of improvements that are more directly pedagogical. In other words, we have to think of establishing general conditions that will give the teacher a chance; and we have to think of what the teacher must do to take that chance. Between these two worlds of general social policy and teaching method lies an area that overlaps with both. Learning is of course overwhelmingly social. The image of the solitary student in his study must not mislead us. Even there he is really communing with other men's thoughts through the book he is reading or preparing to communicate with them through the paper he is writing. Essentially we learn because we are social beings. We have all sorts of experiences of social groups, groups of different kinds and different sizes. What is the effect, not simply on what we learn, but on our capacity to learn, of these experiences of growing up and living in social groupings? The very structure of these groups has an effect on our learning. For

49

instance, in the first and most important social group of which we are part, the family, our capacity for independent initiative in a co-operative setting may turn on the degree to which our upbringing is repressively authoritarian or reasonably permissive. Again, at school the structure of the various groupings into which we fall, and the roles that different people are expected to play, have profound effects. There is the largest single group, the school as a whole. There is the class as a group, and its structure. A study of this might consider the class including the teacher or the class as separate from (as indeed often over and against) the teacher. A teaching method is not just something that you can pick up and apply equally elsewhere. It is something that cannot be separated from the psychological relationship between the teacher and the children. This, to use familiar shorthand terms, may be authoritarian (the teacher not to be challenged or questioned, and "over" rather than "with" the children); or it may be *laisser-faire* (the children left to discover things for themselves, learning—or failing to learn—from their own mistakes); or it may be democratic (the teacher as a friendly counsellor and source of knowledge and to some extent leadership, but "with" rather than "over" the children). Every one of these catch-phrases of course needs analysis, and no one of the methods will work equally well in every kind of society, since home and society on the one hand, and school on the other, cannot be conducted on completely different assumptions as to the relationship of the young with adults. And lastly, children and young people are members of another group, that of their own contemporaries (the "peer-group") and the role and scope that this has in any society has an important effect on education. On all these matters there has been a vast amount of study in recent years by the social psychologists of education. I must leave it here, not because it is not important, but because it concerns the bearing of social groupings on the problems of teaching rather than what we are now discussing, the relationship between social policy and education.

There is a second area of study proper to the social psychologist about which also I shall say little. Some studies of social learning rest on general rather than clinical psychology.[1] But a number of writers, trained in the Freudian or some other school of clinical psychology, have attempted to apply their clinical insights and theories to the wider problems of society. Freud himself had believed that psychoanalytical knowledge could help to elucidate not only the myths and fairy-tales and other expressions of the early social consciousness of mankind, but also our social institutions—religion, morality, law, and philosophy—and civilization itself.[2] Jung, with his concept of the "collective unconscious," offered a similar bridge from the clinic to society at large. This is a tricky matter. Many uncommitted readers feel that to apply what may be fruitful working hypotheses in the clinic to society at large may illuminate some important phenomena but is a good long way from what can be accepted as objective social science. Nevertheless some of these insights into the workings of society, especially in relation to the upbringing of the young and to education, whether brought by adherents of a particular school of psychology or by synthesizers from more than one, have been valuable.

Let me take just one example. Erik Erikson's well-known book *Childhood and Society*[3] is pretty heavily Freudian. Some like it, and some like it less, because of this emphasis. A problem he discusses in one part of the book is what goes wrong with the education of the young Sioux Indians based on their

[1] e.g. BANDURA and WALTERS, *Social Learning and Personality* (New York, Holt, Rinehart & Winston, 1963).

[2] ERNEST JONES, *Sigmund Freud*, vol. II, p. 244 (Hogarth Press, 1955).

[3] Imago Publishing Co., n.d., part 2, Ch. III.

reservation in the southwest corner of South Dakota. They are under the control of the United States Commissioner for Indian Affairs, and there is clearly a conflict between the assumptions of their traditional society before they were driven into the reservation and the assumptions of the modern America into which they might go and that is responsible for their education. Their traditional life had been based on one thing, the buffalo. As Erikson, says, quoting from Wissler—

> When the buffalo died, the Sioux died, ethnically and spiritually. The buffalo's body had provided not only food and material for clothing, covering, and shelter, but such utilities as bags and boats, strings for bows and for sewing, cups and spoons. Medicine and ornaments were made of buffalo parts; his droppings, sun-dried, served as fuel in winter. Societies and seasons, ceremonies and dances, mythology and children's play extolled his name and image.

The ruthless invasion of the whites, destroying not only the buffalo but a whole way of life, was followed by a completely muddled policy towards the Indian, one neither of conquering and assimilating, nor of "leaving be." There was something like a guerrilla war over getting the children into schools. This period was followed by a much more humane and understanding administration. But the result of all this has been to make the Sioux Indian what Erikson calls, taking a term from psychoanalysis, a "compensation neurotic." His sense of security and identity depend on his status as some one to whom something is owed.

This has serious repercussions on the effort to give the Sioux boys and girls education. Increasingly through school there is psychological withdrawal. The schools are physically much more attractive than the Indians' homes and there are rich opportunities for varied interests. But it doesn't seem to work. Erikson brings his psychoanalytical training to bear on this conflict between early childhood training and school education, and on the conflicts set up by the change of *mores*. Most of the children return to their homes in the reservation as offering the best security. They could go out into the white man's world but they have not assimilated the values of that world strongly enough to give them much hope of success. And why should they? They will not be allowed to starve on the reservation. Erikson concludes that the problem cannot be solved until the general problem of the poor white in American society is solved too, for a poor non-white is all that the average Sioux can be. Not, be it noted, from lack of intelligence: the measured intelligence of the average Sioux child is slightly above that of the surrounding whites.

Such studies are of great interest, and may be of great importance, especially where there is a culture-clash of this kind. Such culture-clashes are already a phenomenon of our world as a whole, because of the impact of the white man's technology on pretechnical ways of life. They may be of importance even within a developed society. It is not certain that the kind of explanation Erikson gives in his cited case is the right one; in his Appendix he refers to another view, though he adheres (with some persuasiveness, I think) to his own. There will be more than one general explanation of the phenomenon of psychological withdrawal of groups of our own teenagers from adult society and from the school and its values in their adolescent years.

Having said this and emphasized the interest and possible importance of socio-psychological studies of this type, I want to come back to the main thread of my argument, which concerns the relationship between social and educational policy and in particular the concept of educability. We must now consider what the psychologist has to say about the reserves of ability in our population, the so-called pool of ability, and the concept of measured intelligence in relation to it.

Michael Young's delightful and important moral fable,

The Rise of the Meritocracy[1] graphically illustrates the potential social importance (in this case, the danger) of the psychometrist, the psychologist who can measure intelligence or ability and who is acknowledged by society to be able to do so. The famous formula of that imagined society was, the reader will recall, "I.Q. plus Effort equals Merit." But that implies that one can measure the Intelligence Quotient, and that one knows, moreover what it is that one has measured. Dr. Young's book was written before the present backswing against the over-confident use of the intelligence test for selective purposes, and the formula was near enough to what was happening in our selective school system, and therefore in our society, to be disturbing. Two related tendencies have been observable in recent years: first, rather less confidence in the precision and finality of measurements of intelligence; and second, rather more attention to psychologists who have said that such tests should be used for diagnostic rather than for virtually final selective purposes. These two tendencies have combined with stricter examination of the concept of a limited pool of ability in our population to make us believe that there is a greater scope for justified educational expansion, especially in secondary and higher education, than most people had supposed.

The Robbins Committee found it necessary to go into these questions in order to make reasonable estimates of the degree to which we should expand higher education. Its own research work was statistical, not psychological; but the reader is referred to the section on "The Pool of Ability" constituting Part III of Appendix One of the Committee's Report. This survey itself refers its readers to Professor Philip Vernon's book, *Intelligence and Attainment Tests*[2] for a review of the evidence that measured ability is a function of two variables,

---

[1] Thames and Hudson, 1958.
[2] University of London Press, 1960.

one innate and one coming from the environment, in degrees that it is difficult to establish with precision, though there is almost certainly a larger environmental element than most people had until recently supposed. The Committee said in the body of its Report (paragraph 137)—

Moreover the belief that there exists some easy method of ascertaining an intelligence factor unaffected by education or background is outmoded. Years ago, performance in "general intelligence tests" was thought to be relatively independent of earlier experience. It is now known that in fact it is dependent upon previous experience to a degree sufficiently large to be of great relevance.

I think this is a fair comment on the shift of emphasis that has taken place. There have always been psychologists who have been cautious about the use of such tests. Their originator, Binet, recognized that there was a factor of environment implicit in the findings.[1] Others have always counselled their use as aids to an opinion, especially a diagnostic opinion, rather than their acceptance as something precise and final. The psychologists to whom we owe the development of these tests have on the whole not confused "pure" intelligence with what the tests measured. The tests measured overt capacities, certainly acquired to some extent in the course of experience. But the popular notion has been that intelligence tests have measured an invariable genetic "intelligence," and with considerable precision.[2] And the ranking given to children

[1] See DR. ALICE HEIM, The Appraisal of Intelligence, pp. 19–26 (Methuen, 1954).

[2] This passage owes much to discussion with my friend Dr. W. D. Wall. He has plied me with references to the British Journal of Educational Psychology from 1943 to 1955 to show that psychologists in these years were well aware of the social factors in intelligence. He has no doubt saved me from over-statement, and I am especially grateful for the reference to Sir Cyril Burt's paper in Vol. XLVI, Part II (1947), but I still think an important shift of emphasis has occurred. For an account of this inter-disciplinary dialogue see Professor Wiseman's recent work Education and Environment (Manchester University Press, 1964).

through such tests was almost held to place them with some finality in categories of general ability—a most unsophisticated view. Until quite recently intelligence tests were becoming much too confidently used instruments of educational —and therefore of social—policy. People from teachers to mere visiting speakers at Prize Days who understood what a proper self-confidence and self-respect could do for a boy or girl, and how dangerous was the opposite, had to fight against this very wrong over-categorization and do their best to make the B streams and the C, D, E, and F streams, and the great army of the non-selected, believe in themselves.

The resistances of experience and common sense to the alleged "findings" of research are not always wrong. In this case what teachers and parents know about the potentialities of their non-A-stream young, and (to be fair) what the more cautious and sophisticated psychologists had never denied, now has the support of popular psychology itself. Indeed there is some danger that the reaction may go too far and that we may forget that the tests introduced for selection at eleven plus were good tests (so long as we did not force them into wrong uses), were introduced to promote fairer selection, and are still quite indispensable for counselling and diagnostic purposes.[1]

In the present reaction there is some danger of forgetting that the genetic factor *is* of cardinal importance. It should also be remembered that in a sense the business of a teacher is to falsify a diagnosis, that is to say to bring remedial factors to bear which will make a likely poor result a better one. (This is not to invalidate the evidence that selection at eleven has often been wrong, for there is no reason to suppose that those who do badly at the grammar school are worse taught than those who do well in the modern school.) Our recently

[1] *See* NATIONAL FOUNDATION FOR EDUCATIONAL RESEARCH, *Procedures for the Allocation of Pupils in Secondary Education* (1963).

increased awareness of the importance of differentiating social experience in developing operational intelligence must not drive us to the other extreme so that we forget the genetic factor. It is not true that if we had perfect social equality we should all be equally intelligent, and it is not to be assumed that in a perfect society the best way for every young person to spend the years between eighteen and twenty-one would be in a university. The key points are two: first, that any reservoir of potential ability is at present limited, not merely by genetic factors but by social experience that it is in our power to modify; and second that there is no limit to such potential so near as to prevent us from expanding our upper secondary and higher education much more than at present.

The notion that because students in the sixth form, or in universities, have an I.Q. of a given figure or above, and because the distribution of intelligence is such that only a small percentage of the population will have such an I.Q., therefore there is a limit of this size to the number in the population suitable for such a level of education, has now been discredited. Referring to this argument, Professor Vernon said in a paper written for the Robbins Committee[1]—

> I wish to state categorically that this reasoning is unsound, and that no calculations of the numbers of eligible students can be based on tests of intelligence or other aptitudes, though they could conceivably be based on tests or surveys of aspirations, interests, and social attitudes in the population.

On the contrary, he says—

> The main factors in the supply of suitable students would appear to be—
> (i) The educational and vocational aspirations of the family; its expectation that the children will undertake an arduous

[1] Printed in *The Sociological Review*, no. 7, ed. PAUL HALMOS (University of Keele, 1963).

educational career and eventually enter high-level jobs, and the material and moral support it provides towards these ends,

(ii) the child's own drives, interests, and ideals,

(iii) the traditions and current attitudes in the schools the child attends, and in society generally, and the prestige of occupations requiring university (or other higher institutional) training,

(iv) the effectiveness of teachers and teaching methods in developing favourable attitudes among pupils towards, and attainments in, the academic subjects and education generally.

I must say that, for myself, I have always known this and for a very simple reason. There are considerable numbers of boys and girls who have "failed the eleven plus" but whose correspondence with these criteria of Professor Vernon's has been close and whose parents have been able to send them to schools in the private sector and then on into higher or professional education. They are now doing perfectly well as educated and professionally trained men and women of a kind which it had been adjudged that they could not become when small boys and girls under our selection tests. Many teachers and parents no doubt have felt the same way in these dark meritocratic years, but only impressionistically. To have the weight of professional evidence put in the same scale is of great importance. No doubt, however, it will take some time for the principles Professor Vernon has outlined to be assimilated into our general practice. Few things could be more important.

There is one particular observation that deserves notice: that the effects of different kinds of environment, and the role of education itself as a determinant of the growth of intelligence, *increase* as one goes up the age-scale from primary to higher education. Let me quote Vernon once again—

> Heterogeneity of environment begins to increase when children are segregated into different types of secondary schools and after they leave school. Hence its effects are more noticeable in the 'teens, when children are at the stage of acquiring the more complex

concepts and modes of thinking. From 15 to 20, indeed, educational stimulation differs so widely from one person to another that it becomes the major determinant of further growth in intelligence. And when we go outside a single culture, the variations in concepts, habits of thought and in attitudes to intellectual tasks are so wide that useful comparisons can no longer be made by any intelligence tests.[1]

It takes little imagination to see that the difference between an educational policy for secondary and higher education based on such findings and one based on the vulgar notion that because only two and a quarter per cent of the population have I.Q.s of 130 or over therefore the university population is already if anything too large, is total.

The carefully analysed evidence as to the "pool of ability" marshalled in the Robbins Report and its first Appendix has probably produced a greater change in a concept basic to educational policy-making than any but the most original works of scholarship. Before the Report almost every one accepted the metaphor. After the Report had been published critics who still relied on it were simply asked: "Have you read Appendix One?" Professor Vernon, summarizing the paper that he wrote for the Committee, began—

> This paper contests the view—widespread among educationists—that there exists in the population a fixed distribution or "pool" of intelligence, which limits either the numbers of individuals capable of higher education, or the educational standards that can be achieved by groups of pupils or students of given I.Q. level.

The view is already not widespread. What is interesting is how it came to be so.

The first thing that struck those who had to answer the critics who invoked this metaphor was that they had not noticed a very simple thing: that the population was increasing. It stands to reason that if this is so you have, so to speak, to run hard to keep in the same place. The "pool" has increased for a demographic reason. The number of eighteen-year-olds in Great Britain in 1955 was 642,000. The number in 1965 is 963,000. This of course reflects the jump in the number of births after the last war, but it shows that the demand by qualified students for higher education in 1965 was bound to be far greater, from this cause alone, than it was in 1955, and without any lowering of standards. But after the tapering off, following the passing through of the bulge, forecasts suggest that there will be a rise again and that we shall reach almost the same peak figure by 1981 (actually, 933,000). The fact that so many critics of expansion had overlooked so simple a demographic fact shows how powerful a metaphor can be. Half-realizing this, no doubt, the Robbins Report tried to get a different and better metaphor into circulation, that of the widow's cruse; but it failed. (Fewer people read the Bible these days.)

The second oddity was that many dons hadn't allowed for the "trend" any more than they had allowed for the "bulge." The trend referred to is, of course, that of staying on longer in the secondary school, giving a greater pool of entrants from which the universities could draw. In eight years, from 1954 to 1962, the percentage of seventeen-year-olds at school grew from 7·9 to 12. There are some factors suggesting that the trend will be steeper still in the coming years, others that it may be less steep; and the Report took the middle assumption that it would increase at the same rate (till 1980) as over these eight years. To parody Michael Young, "Trend plus Bulge equals Expansion"; and there is no getting away from it.

There is no obvious reason for supposing that expansion because of these factors would lead to a lowering of quality among students in higher education. There has not been a lowering of standard as far as one can tell in recent years although numbers have grown. In fact, the Report says, "wastage" (failure to complete a course successfully) has been less than it was in the early 1950s. And degree results (in so far as they can give a reliable picture) show an improvement at all levels except at the very top, where one would not expect it.

Of course there must be a limit somewhere. It is most unlikely that there will ever be a time when all the population will stay in formal education till the age of twenty-one (in some American states, though, they are approaching the half way mark). What the Robbins Committee said confidently, so far as the degree of expansion they recommended was concerned, was that there was no reason for fearing a shortage of properly qualified entrants. In terms of their proposals it was not even necessary to rely on the kind of arguments Professor Vernon adduced, indicating all the possibilities attendant upon social and cultural influences producing a higher operational intelligence at the age of eighteen.

How then can the university teachers who do have sincere doubts about expansion have got into their frame of mind? I think there are two reasons we should look at. One is not anything to do with psychological evidence, though it is very much to do with the function of universities. Some dons, having very distinguished academic records themselves, come to feel that any work below that of at least a high second-class degree is not really university work at all, and that students who cannot attain this level are not of university quality. One could talk about this (I think it is quite wrong) but it is perhaps enough to say two things. First, that this would be a completely new principle. Oxford and Cambridge until very recent times have had great numbers of young gentle-men in residence who were not scholars in this sense at all, and it is a little absurd for a university itself to deny that any student who has secured one of its degrees (even a pass degree) has not been adjudged by the university itself to have completed the course, maybe not with brilliance, but at least successfully. The second point is that many such young men, leaving out those who really have wasted their time, have gained something from the university that later they would never wish to have been without, even though they barely achieved their double thirds.

The second reason for the doubts of some dons is, however, more relevant to the present stage of this discussion. They see their entrants as they are just before the age of entry. It may be true that at that age the young man or woman they interview may not seem very likely undergraduate timber. But if they are judging in broader terms whether we could have a larger proportion of an age-group in the universities they must think of all the possible improvements that might increase the proportion *before* the age of eighteen. As Dr. C. M. Fleming said in her review of work in social psychology that had bearings on education, "There are much stronger grounds now than even twenty years ago for a belief in human educability."[1] And that was twenty more years ago.

Of course it is not reasonable to suppose that every would-be entrant to an educational institution should be admitted because he thinks he would like it, or even seriously desires it. There will always be young men and women who would like to enter the university and who will be reasonably judged not to be suitable. What we now understand, however—and this is new—is that demand to enter is itself one factor in suitability to do so. If there are two boys, one from the home of a doctor or lawyer and who early conceives the thought of following in his father's footsteps and is encouraged to do so, and the other the son of parents who do not much value education and who is not greatly interested himself in going to a university, and if the measured intelligence of these two

[1] C. M. FLEMING, *The Social Psychology of Education*, p. 58 (Kegan Paul, 1944).

boys is the same at thirteen or fourteen and rather borderline for university possibilities, then the odds are high that the first boy will get to the university and do well enough to justify it, and that the second boy will not. This will not have depended just on "I.Q." These different kinds of experience resulting in a different order of demand for education and professional careers, will themselves have affected the "I.Q." The differences in motivations, values, and attitudes will have started virtually from birth, have been greatly accentuated as soon as language began, and have become greater all the way up.

To sum up, then, the psychological determinants of our present thinking about education and society. We do have an increasing insight into the importance for learning of the experiences of social relations and social groupings of all kinds from early childhood onwards. We are increasingly sensitive to the effect of large-scale social dislocations and clashes of cultural norms on readiness and ability to learn. But, apart from these matters, we realize that the development of an effective operational intelligence is much more dependent on social factors than we had supposed, and we know that the assumption that there is a genetically fixed pool of ability such as to deprive us of good students in a much expanded system of education is no longer tenable.

As with my discussion of the role of sociology in our educational thinking I have taken my examples from the problems that exercise us now, in the mid 1960s. I have done this because these are our immediate problems and because psychological studies have in these recent years necessitated a major shift in some of our dominant assumptions. But, once again, these are only examples of a general point, valid when the examples themselves will have the dust of history on them. This is that thorough and objective psychological research, like thorough and objective sociological research, is indispensable for our thinking about education and society.

But is this enough? In 1944 we said we wanted to give all children an equal chance, according to their age, aptitude and ability. The sociologists and the psychologists (allies in spite of their professional doubts of each other, like the army and the navy in wartime) now combine to say that we cannot do this without more radical action than we thought necessary. Do we value the principle of educational equality enough to take that action, or is it so radical that we now withdraw from the principle? This is a value question, and we must therefore now turn to studies that can clarify what value judgements are.

IV

PHILOSOPHICAL

WE have seen in what ways sociological and psychological studies can contribute to our thinking about education and society. We have also noted that in so far as they are sciences they cannot be expected to tell us what we ought to do. Philosophy does not claim to be a science at all, in the way in which we use that word in English. There is no corpus of knowledge marshalled in the light of tested theories that we can call Philosophy. Philosophy is a technique for thinking, and is especially concerned with examining our assumptions and defining our concepts. Social philosophy and the philosophy of education are concerned with the assumptions we make and the concepts we use in thinking about society and education. Philosophers are interested in the meanings of the word "ought," and if we say that something ought to be done in education it is as useful to understand what we mean by the word "ought" here as it would be in any other field in which we might use it. But many contemporary philosophers would stop there. They would not go on to say even in general terms what we should do, feeling that that is rather the province of the moralist or of the policy maker. Equally they will consider it to be within their province to say what they think the meanings of the term "values" are, but not to prescribe for us in any overt way what our values should be. In this section, therefore, we might look first at this agreed function of social and educational philosophy, the clarification of our terms. After that we might consider whether the moralist is to be ruled out of court. Lastly we might examine the idea of "values" and consider whether discussion of our social and educational values can be rational, or at least useful.

It is obviously desirable to scrutinize the concepts we invoke so freely when talking about education and society. If we speak of the right of parents to have their children brought up in their own religion, what do we mean when we use the word "right?" What, for that matter, is our conception of a society, and how far is it compatible with separate interests? A Scottish Prime Minister, shocked into forgetfulness of his origins by his opponents' talk of class divisions, exclaimed: "We're all Englishmen, aren't we?" Do we say that the idea of a society is imperfectly realized where there are serious class divisions, or that the idea of a society transcends class divisions? We have already seen that recent work in sociology and psychology is forcing us to think more carefully about the concept of equality of opportunity in education. How does this affect our concept of equality itself? The tripartite scheme of secondary education in this country has been defended by saying: "We aren't all equal, and although this is a hard lesson to learn for all of us there's no great harm in getting children to adjust to these differences early." Is the conception of equality behind such a statement the same as the one we have when, for instance, we say that all citizens should be equal before the law? And if not, is the statement valid as a defence of the tripartite system? The analysis of terms like these is a most important function of the philosopher of education.

Now we can study that subject and have its discipline behind us when we make practical decisions. Or, obversely, we may have to analyse a practical difficulty and be led, whether we quite realize it or not, into the exercise of examining our terms. I should like to give an example of each of these processes.

There is an interesting analysis of "Equality" in *Social*

Principles and the Democratic State by S. I. Benn and R. S. Peters.[1] They have no difficulty in showing that when it is said, with reference to the social and political consideration people should have, that all men are equal, nobody means that they are equally gifted any more than that they are equally tall. We may mean that they have some positive quality, simply as human beings, that justifies their being put into a single category. What, say those writers, is this fundamental human quality? It is rather difficult to find this and isolate it from all particular qualities; so they reject this defence of equality. The phrase "Human Nature" indicates a varying potentiality for a limited range of qualities; it does not indicate some quality that men possess equally and on account of which they should therefore be treated equally. The point is not that they do not, as men, have some common characteristics and common needs, but that they do not have these equally enough to establish that they should be treated equally. Logically, no doubt, this keeps the Benn and Peters case clear of the kind of consideration advanced by an anthropologist like Kluckhohn,[2] who is concerned to refute the extreme cultural relativism of Ruth Benedict and emphasizes that for all the differences between cultures human beings are human beings the world over, and goes on to say: "Ethical universals are the product of universal human nature, which is based, in turn, upon a common biology, psychology and generalized situation."[2] Though if one is impressed by what men have in common one does have a little more sympathy for this defence of equality that Benn and Peters reject. But let us admit their point.

They go on to argue that it is self-defeating to take a prescriptive statement like "all men are equal" in a way that makes

---

[1] Allen and Unwin, 1959, p. 108 ff.

[2] CLYDE KLUCKHOHN: *Culture and Behaviour*, essays 16 and 17 (Free Press of Glencoe, 1962).

its validity turn on the truth of the statement "all men are equal" used descriptively. The prescription needs to be re-formulated. What we really mean when we say that all men are equal is that "none shall be held to have a claim to better treatment than another, in advance of good grounds being produced." "The only rational ground for treating men differently is that they differ in some way that is relevant to the distinction we propose to make." This position can be defended in terms of what we know ourselves to mean by morality, and in particular by impartiality.[1] Such a defence does not logically follow from an analysis of the concepts: it has to be established in its own right. But it can hardly start till confusion over the concepts has been got out of the way. Most popular discussions about equality still suffer from this confusion between the descriptive and the prescriptive, though in practice we do see that unequal cases demand unequal treatment.

We are willing to spend more, if it is necessary, on the education of a handicapped child than on the education of a child who is not handicapped. We recognize that unequal treatment (in the sense of spending more than the average) is necessary in the interests of equality itself. The same principle must apply at the other end of the scale. The education of the future doctor or research scientist is bound to cost more than the education of the future technician; but again this is justified inequality, for a greater than average expenditure is necessary if these young people are to have an equal chance of realizing their potentialities, and also to be of appropriate service to society. What does complicate the question here, however, is that there will also be a personal gain to these more gifted young people: they will be virtually certain to end up in a higher income bracket because of the extra expenditure from public funds on their education. This is the justification for the

[1] *See* BENN and PETERS, Ch. II.

proposal that some of the support for their education might well be in the form of loans, repayable according to the incomes they ultimately earn.

Now, however, let us look at this question the other way, not at the usefulness of thought-out general concepts when we come on practical situations, but at the way in which a practical situation may drive us to think out our concepts and perhaps to redefine them in terms of changing circumstances.

In this country we have placed a high value on the academic freedom of the universities. But increasingly we have felt the need for the work of the universities to be more explicitly related to the national interests, social and economic, to be developed with more coherence as a whole, and to be so co-ordinated that the large public funds now devoted to it are not wastefully spent. How is the claim to academic freedom to be related to the need for national planning of higher education? To answer this practical question we have to ask what justifies the claim to academic freedom, and in particular to ask whether it can be accepted as a blanket term covering all sorts of immunities. Can we distinguish the indispensable academic freedoms from other immunities that, however agreeable to the beneficiaries, are not really indispensable to our proper aims?

The academic freedom that our universities have enjoyed did not originate from a deliberate decision by a liberal-minded state. Its origin is in the historic fact that the universities were private institutions. The one sign that there was a public interest was in the fact that their existence was sanctioned by a Royal Charter, and this justifies a Royal Commission whenever the public interest is held to make that necessary. But this is mere formality. We know that they are an indispensable part of the public realm. And indeed, despite academic conservatism they have been reasonably responsive to social needs articulated by government or quasi-governmental organs, and the device of the University Grants Committee has enabled public funds accorded them in large sums to be responsibly deployed without any governmental encroachment on their freedom. But we are now moving into a somewhat different era. We are conscious of great needs and of limited resources. The desirability of at least a greater degree of planning than in the past is generally accepted. The proper concern about resolving the possible incompatibility of national planning of university activities and academic freedom is compelling us to examine this term and to ask what are the mere historical accidents and what are the still quite necessary academic freedoms?

There is a chapter on this subject in the Robbins Report (Chapter XVI) and there is no need here to repeat that Report's recommendations. But there is interest in noting the kind of exercise that led to them and the kind of principle that informs them. As has been seen, this had to be an exercise in the reconciliation of rights, each of which had its own validity. And it was a reconciliation that had to be made, not simply in terms of abstract principles, but in terms of a changed social situation. But one cannot read the relevant chapter of the Report without seeing also that it is written by people who hold to certain values, the grounds for which they have tried to examine. They agree that the arrangements made for the universities are of proper concern to society as a whole, and at the same time they agree that certain kinds of pressure on the universities by the state can jeopardize the freely exercised intellectual leadership which characterizes the contribution of the universities to society. (One definition of a right is that it is a claim without whose recognition associations or individuals cannot discharge their essential functions in society.) Implicitly, rather than explicitly, such a practical point of policy drives us back on the assumptions of our social philosophy.

It is clear that the writers of the Report do not believe in a monolithic society but in a pluralist one: that is to say a society in which the state or a single party is not the direct and only source of authority. They believe that in an open pluralist society there is scope for accommodation between interests that seem to be opposed; for this appropriate machinery is necessary, but it takes place largely by discussion (no doubt backed by strength, but not too overtly or roughly) and this discussion leads to a recognition of some particular immunities in a context of understanding by the beneficiaries of the interests of society as a whole. From such assumptions, and from a re-examination of the concept of academic freedom in the light of them, the recommendations follow. The Committee believed that academic freedom is not separable from a large degree of devolution of financial and administrative autonomy to each university once the broad national interests are assured. They saw freedom to appoint staff, to decide on the contents of curricula and standards, and to admit students (so long as there is no discrimination extraneous to academic considerations) as being essential academic freedoms. But there must be a reasonably coherent development policy for the universities in the country as a whole, and it would not be reasonable for a university to claim unrestricted power to decide its own development without reference to this when it gets the money for it from public funds.

Cases differ, of course; but this exercise indicates the general procedure and the general emphasis that most people in our society would favour in the much larger task of the general reconciliation of freedom, personal and corporate, with planning. We start with a problem of policy, but in the course of serious discussion we have to become conscious of (and if necessary to question and test) the assumptions of our social philosophy.

As will be seen from this example, analysis of concepts is

necessary, but mere analysis would only help us in a very limited way in deciding what we ought to do. While some writers on ethics would still consider "what ought we to do?" as its central question, the merely analytic philosopher would not go so far. But while we confine them to so austere a diet the hungry sheep look up and are not fed. No doubt it is legitimate for the merely analytical philosopher to turn away and say he is not that kind of shepherd; he is just a trainer helping us not to bleat so incoherently. But it used not to be like this. Philosophers who have written about education from Plato downwards have considered it part of their calling to say in terms of principle what we ought to do. Indeed one can feel sure that any one in this country addressing himself to the problem of academic freedom would have Locke and John Stuart Mill at the back of his mind, setting a framework of reference even though their attitudes did not content him now. And down to John Dewey, one might say, the educational writings of philosophers and their philosophical writing have been all of a piece. You just cannot disentangle them in *The Republic*. No doubt we cannot and should not ignore the immediate heritage in philosophy. It is true that if a writer on education and society is trying to persuade us of a course of action he may not be as objective in his statements of the meaning of terms as he ought to be. Yet the philosopher, like the sociologist, is likely to find himself in front of a mixed situation. He may accept this, and agree that ethical discussion may reasonably go beyond mere analysis, or he may prefer to leave such a development of interest to the moralist. I think the devaluation of metaphysics of recent years has had a carry-over effect here that is not altogether justified.

Consider, for instance, Professor O'Connor's argument for the restricted role of philosophy. He notes that the word philosophy does indeed promise so much more to many people than the negative virtues of clarity, order and antisepsis. But we should know now (he says) that the promise cannot be fulfilled. Metaphysics will not do. He says a statement is metaphysical "if it assumes the existence of entities or facts which lie outside the range of human observation and experience" and that "an argument is metaphysical if it purports to prove the existence of such entities or facts."[1] For twenty-five centuries some of the ablest men have been trying to work out metaphysical views of the universe and man's place in it, and they have failed to give us any agreed positive answer. Metaphysics, he says, cannot give such answers to disputed questions of religion and morality.[2] O'Connor's mind is clearly on metaphysics and religion much more than on morality. The philosophical discussion of morality is not to be dismissed. But the philosopher who is concerned with it need not rely on metaphysics; nor need he, to be useful, be under a compulsion to find answers that are "positive" in the sense in which science is positive.

There is now of course a diminution of the extremer subjectivist or relativist interpretation of "ought" statements. Professor C. L. Stevenson, whose *Ethics and Language*[3] was widely taken to be a modulated expression of such a position, argues in a later book[4] that, although the misunderstanding may have been his own fault to some extent, his theory was not a merely relativist one. He makes a distinction that is very germane to our present discussion—

A social scientist attempts to survey people's evaluations with a temporary detachment—to survey them without as yet taking sides, and thus without as yet participating in the normative issues that they may occasion. So *his* problem is basically different from the problem he describes. His problem, in short, is concerned with

[1] *An Introduction to the Philosophy of Education*, p. 17.
[2] ibid., p. 113.
[3] Yale University Press, 1944.
[4] *Facts and Values*, p. 92 (Yale, 1963).

what is *considered* good, whereas the problem that he describes is concerned with what *is* good.

This brings Stevenson very close to the position of Dr. Toulmin, his former appreciative critic, for Toulmin makes just this point that when you say "this is good" you are not merely saying "I like this and want to persuade you to like it too," but "this is worthy of approval." In other words you are maintaining that there is reason for saying it is good, and so for approving it, and so for recommending others to do so.[1]

As Stevenson says, to confuse these two problems may be very tempting to the sociologist. An analytical philosopher might say that to confuse the two problems has proved irresistible to most philosophers in the past. Personally (as I have said for the sociologist) I have no objection to their writing about both, though of course I don't want them to be confused. What I am certain of is that the second should be written about as well as the first, and by trained academic people as well as politicians and journalists. The question is whether this can be done on the plane of rationality, or if you like of theory. As we have seen, Professor O'Connor thinks that theory is at best a courtesy title when applied to education; Mr. Hirst is more hopeful. The former's difficulty is that for him a theory has to be "positive," as in science. I would come near to Mr. Hirst's position and say that there can be discussion that, if not leading to theories, is at least theoretical (i.e. an attempt to subsume experience in general statements), although not admitting of "positive" answers. There seems to me no paradox here, but a simple need to understand a kind of discussion that is neither metaphysical nor scientific, and that is in fact perfectly familiar.

There is a whole range of studies which can never be "positive" in the sense of giving certain answers on the basis

[1] STEPHEN TOULMIN, *Reason in Ethics*, Ch. 3 (Cambridge, 1950).

of observed facts, yet which are eminently proper and lead to acceptable conclusions. If I may refer to my own experience, I was decisively brought to this view by a lecture I heard by Dr. F. R. Leavis when I was an undergraduate at Cambridge. He was discussing the nature of literary criticism. He argued that it was not and never could be a science, but that it was equally absurd to go to the other extreme and say it was all a matter of personal taste about which discussion was value-less. The literary critic appeals to norms of human experience. We discuss a book or a play in order to share our experiences, on the assumption that in large measure (though not neces-sarily in totality) they can be shared. We have all had our eyes opened to the merit of a work of literature through such discussions. The possibility is there because we have eyes. We simply had not looked before in the right direction. It is in this way that our taste is formed. We learn to discriminate not only between what is good and less good in literature but between different kinds of satisfaction, and (as Mr. T. S. Eliot said was so necessary) we learn to expect from this or that kind of poetry the particular kind of satisfaction, and not others, that it may be expected to give.

Such discussions are never final. The powers of perception of different people, and their balance of interests, vary. Conclusions that are generally accepted now may not be accepted in a gener-ation's time. But they vary about human norms, not anarchi-cally in a void where there are no criteria at all. That is why, after fashion has had its fling, we can speak of an established writer. The greatest difficulty is across the dividing lines of different cultures. It is notoriously difficult for an Englishman justly to appreciate Racine, "justly" as that would be inter-preted by a Frenchman. The French have done rather better by Shakespeare. But it is still an odd experience for an English-man to watch a production of a Shakespeare play in a French theatre, especially if it is given by an English company. The least instructed in the audience are unhappy that it is not Racine or Corneille. The more instructed know that it is not, and, therefore, assume it must be like Victor Hugo. It takes a Frenchman of catholic culture to understand that Shakespeare is neither classic or romantic in the French sense of these terms, but has his own modes. Yet, even so, no educated man of any country doubts the greatness of Shakespeare.

Philosophy relies much more on argument than literary criticism and less on the illustration that wins unargued agreement. But the two are alike in not being positivist. And the literary critic and the moral philosopher are both prescriptive writers, telling us what they believe to be good, to be worthy of a high valuation. If we have learned from critical discussion of literature and the arts, surely it is also the experience of most of us that we have learned from those who have written passionately of what they believe to be good in society and in education. It might even be argued that just as an anthropologist cannot understand a society or its behaviour without a certain "internal" comprehension, so one cannot judge the force of a plea for greater recognition of a given value in society without such strongly felt exposition. The virtue of such a strongly felt exposition, so long as it is reasonable and not fanatical, is that one can see how important certain values are even though on balance one may disagree with an author's conclusion. For instance, a strong plea for the qualities that a writer believes to depend on a minority or *élite* culture may well be illuminating even for those who would dispute the social conclusion. Similarly, many readers have gained insight from reading a book like Tawney's *Equality* even though they were unlikely themselves ever to vote socialist.

It is doubtful if this kind of insight will ever be gained from colder analyses of concepts. When Tawney died Hugh Gaitskell said:[1] "It seems to me that what gave them [his books]

[1] At the memorial service at St. Martin in the Fields, February 8th, 1962.

their special quality was the way they combined learning with passion." And he went on to refer explicitly to *The Acquisitive Society* and *Equality*—

> These books combined passion and learning. There was nothing false or exaggerated in them. In exposing the contrast between the Christian ethic and the actual condition of society, Tawney was drawing aside the veil and showing us what existed behind it. He was not inventing things, but simply showing them to us—things we had failed to appreciate before, but which we recognized immediately he wrote about them.

The point I want to make is that the reader's understanding of the importance of the scale of values Tawney was recommending depends on the kind of language—most certainly non-scientific language—that he used—

> A nation is not civilized because a handful of its members are successful in acquiring large sums of money and in persuading their fellows that a catastrophe will occur if they do not acquire it, any more than Dahomey was civilized because its king had a golden stool and an army of slaves, or Judea because Solomon possessed a thousand wives and imported apes and peacocks, and surrounded the worship of Moloch and Ashtaroth with an impressive ritual. What matters to a society is less what it owns than what it is and how it uses its possessions.[1]

He is a master of irony and uses it to bring his point home—

> It is the nature of privilege and tyranny to be unconscious of themselves, and to protest, when challenged, that their horns and hooves are not dangerous, as in the past, but useful and handsome decorations, which no self-respecting society would dream of dispensing with.[2]

And he can rise to scorn. We have already shown how inadequate the concept of equality of opportunity is proving

[1] R. H. TAWNEY, *Equality*, p. 103 (Allen and Unwin, 1931).
[2] ibid., p. 118.

in our educational arrangements. But one must go to Tawney to understand its function ("Most social systems need a lightning conductor. The formula which supplies it to our own is equality of opportunity"[1]) and its miserable in-adequacy—

> It is possible that intelligent tadpoles reconcile themselves to the inconveniences of their position, by reflecting that, though most of them will live and die as tadpoles and nothing more, the more fortunate of the species will one day shed their tails, distend their mouths and stomachs, hop nimbly on to dry land, and croak ad-dresses to their former friends on the virtues by means of which tadpoles of character and capacity can rise to be frogs.[2]

Not philosophy? No, it is not. But if we had not heard Tawney a voice would have been missing from the conversation.

There is nothing really mysterious about the concept of values. Tawney discusses them at a high level, but in much less momentous matters we all form our sense of what is more and what is less important, and in the practical world, strike our working balance. We reflect upon our experience, discuss it with other people, and gradually come to a realization of what we value most. Take, for instance, the question as to the desirability or otherwise of moving out of a traditional work-ing-class neighbourhood to a suburban housing estate. What do young married people who have such an opportunity do? They find out the facts, of course: comparative rents, distance from work, chances of a good school for their children, and so on. And they talk it over, with some of their friends who have made such a move and with their families who may well be staying put. These talks help them to think of some things they might have overlooked, for instance that they will be very much on their own in the new council house and iso-

[1] R. H. TAWNEY, *Equality*, p. 138 (Allen and Unwin, 1931).
[2] ibid., p. 142.

lated from the warm and friendly life of their own extended families and their friends. It won't be so easy to rally the grannies. The football match with dad on Saturday afternoon, the circle at the pub on Saturday evening, the call over the wall for some neighbourly help from Mrs. Jones: what do these things add up to compared with a better house, a better neighbourhood, a new infant school for the children? People make their different choices, one way or the other, to their satisfaction or their regret.

In principle the decisions we make collectively about the society we live in are just the same. Would we sooner the rates went up so that we could have a new school, or would we sooner have the money for our personal expenditure? Would we sooner make such private provision as we can for medical attention or have a national health service that still has to be paid for, but collectively? If we think out our answers to such questions we soon find that we are forming certain general attitudes about the kind of society we favour, and the kind that we do not. Life never being simple, these attitudes are usually the resultant of a kind of thought-out balance. For instance, we want some range of choice in the goods we buy: more than one brand of a given article, and more than one kind of article in a range not all of which we might want or be able to afford. But we know that there are economies in uniform large-scale production. During the war we were content to have a limited range of things in the same general class because only so could we have them at a reasonable price (and only so could the nation have them without too much expenditure of energy and money on consumer goods). If there was a government guarantee of standards in these articles we thought, in the circumstances, that this was the right policy for the country.

Now when this thinking about preferences reaches a point where we know there are some qualities we should put very high indeed, so much so that we should feel deeply offended if they were ignored or destroyed, we begin to speak of our social values. There are some people who believe that the railways ought to be run as a business. There are others who say they should be run as a public service, with a subsidy if necessary. This is not a question as to whether you want the railways to run at a profit or at a loss: that is a silly way of putting it. The proper question is like the one about the rates and the new school: do you want the railways to be paid for entirely by fares and freight charges, or do you think that in part we should pay for them collectively, through a tax-supported subsidy? In discussing this question we soon find that we are considering more than economics. People take sides over this according to the kind of society that they want. Those who say the railways should support themselves by fares and freight charges feel deeply offended, in terms of principle, when they see a headline: "Railways make a loss again." Those who say they should be thought of as a public service feel equally offended when they see a headline: "Beeching closes ten more lines in rural Scotland."

Or take another example. Some people feel that they ought to be allowed to buy land and put a building on it with the minimum of restrictions. And they do not much mind if others do the same. They won't much mind even if a public authority does it. Pylons may disfigure the Downs, but if we don't put them up, how can we possibly have enough cheap electricity? Others are up in arms (though usually too late) when a grove of fine trees is felled, or when the lovely line of a village street is being spoiled by some obtrusive building that wrecks its harmony. They protest that this country is losing all sense of civilized values; and the difference is indeed between people who have different social values, that is to say different settled principles as to the relative importance of different things. But we are not content to acknowledge a difference and leave it there. We write letters to the papers. There are indignation meetings. There are questions to Members of Parliament and questions by Members of Parliament. Such discussions make us all think more actively as to what we are doing: is the kind of society we are allowing to come into being the kind of society we really desire? This means not merely that we think about our social values, but that we modify them as discussion enables us to see more clearly.

What I have been saying is not a detour from the subject of education and its relationship with society. If our society is to be good it must nourish sound and civilized values in the young. It is, therefore, not surprising that the word "values" is often on the lips of those who speak, write, and admonish us about education. Unfortunately this word is one of the most carelessly used in the educationist's vocabulary. It has great knock-down virtue in an argument, especially if one can claim an Absolute as an ally. The concept of Absolute Values is very acceptable to those for whom the idea of God has become more of a philosophical than a personal reality, and the overtones of the phrase are intended to be awe-inspiring. However, we can note how the word "values" is used in ordinary discourse and how fruitful discussion of values may be without entering into the controversial question as to whether the origin of our values is in some "Absolute" beyond our experience or in our experience itself. That is why I have deliberately used an unpretentious approach to the meaning of the word, showing its use in common language.

This is the central idea to hold on to in the discussion of values, that they are moral or social qualities to which we attach relative importance, and that when we are speaking of very important values we refer to qualities that we should feel deeply offended to see ignored or destroyed. This would of course be only the beginning of a systematic analysis of the possible meanings of the word. Such a systematic analysis is given very clearly by Professor Arnaud Reid in the third chapter of his book, *Philosophy and Education*.[1] But if, as Mr. Richard Robinson argues,[2] a decision as to what is good is a matter of choice and neither of scientific nor of supposed metaphysical fact, the choice is something that we can discuss in terms of norms of human experience. In the discussion we rely on the norms, though we know that there will always be variations from them, just as we may in discussing works of literature and art. It is important to a society that such discussions, about social values and about the arts, should be general and of a serious critical level. Without this it is not possible to have a civilized society.

It is interesting to note that C. L. Stevenson, after the most ingenious analysis of innumerable examples of forms of ethical statement, himself comes back to what looks, to a non-philosopher, suspiciously like common sense. In the fifth essay in his *Facts and Values* he discusses the difficulty of justifying evaluative statements by reasons alone. If we do agree that a reason, if true, would help to justify an evaluative conclusion, then in saying that we are really making another value judgement of our own. If, for instance, an absolute pacifist says that we must avoid war even at the cost of losing our freedom, because a nuclear war would destroy millions of people, we may come to the conclusion that his reason is "true" (that is to say that a nuclear war would destroy millions of lives). But we are still left with a value judgement to make ourselves, as to which would be worse, to have millions of people killed or to lose our freedom. And however long we go on with these reductions to reasons we shall always have a residual value judgement to make. So it seems as if we are left with nothing but scepticism as to the possibility of justi-

[1] Heinemann, 1962. *See also* TOULMIN, op. cit., Part III, Ch. 11.
[2] *An Atheist's Values*, section I.4 (Oxford, 1964).

fying our value judgements. But haven't we started on the problem, says Stevenson, at the wrong end? "Why cannot we start as we do in common life? There we have attitudes that we initially trust and we proceed to express them. Reasons serve not to bring our attitudes into being but only to redirect them. And if in accepting or rejecting the reasons we are making new evaluations, and thus expressing new attitudes, that is only to say that more of our attitudes, through the mediation of the reasons, are coming into play."[1] This is surely right. Let us look at our own present value choices, and those of our society, and in the light of reasoned examination of our preferences see how far we wish to reinforce and how far to modify them.

I have dwelt on this question so much because it is of such importance for education in its social setting, especially in a period of rapid change and the perpetual call for attention to values. Our attitudes in this matter are crucial for all that side of education that is concerned with the "socialization" of the young: with the training of character, the making of good citizens, and helping them in general to become useful and acceptable members of society. The bearing of philosophical considerations of the kind we have discussed may seem to be less direct than that of the sociological and psychological considerations discussed earlier, but although we may not be in any strict sense students of philosophy we shall have to think philosophically about many of the problems of education and society if we are to be reasonably sure of our ground.

In the abstract we might say: let us imagine a society that embodies our most cherished values and then devise an education appropriate to it. That of course is what Plato did in *The Republic*. And in the face of so great an example it might seem rash to say that the attempt must be profitless. That would be the wrong word. That no Utopia would be fit

[1] p. 90.

to live in is too easy a jeer. There may be virtue in dreaming out our dreams of the ideal society even though we know we are in the realm of dreams. What would be fatal would be not to know that we were distorting: distorting the realities of the world we live in, and distorting human nature as well. Terrible things can happen to children, as they can to adult human beings, if their lives are controlled by persons with rigid ideal systems in their minds that take no account of the realities of the world and of the needs of human nature. John Stuart Mill's famous account of his education on utilitarian principles is an example of the one; the repressive régimes of Savonarola in Florence and of Calvin in Geneva are examples of the other. Burke was no doubt a "reactionary" and Tom Paine's dismissal of his sentimentality about the *ancien régime* in France was about as final as a single sentence dismissal of a case can ever have been; but Burke's respect for experience, and distrust of those who are merely doctrinaire in the face of it, has a virtue that transcends the party lines of any particular dispute. Those who are concerned with policy, with what we ought to do, will be wiser to start with our present society, and with our people as we know them, in flesh and blood, now; to recognize what have been their distinctive values; and then to reflect and to discuss, so as to fortify the values we respect and to give greater scope to those we feel to have been unduly neglected. As Stevenson says: to start as we do in common life, with attitudes that we initially trust, though we may modify them as reasoning shows to be desirable.

We start this way in education. We bring the young up in a social tradition and we impress its values upon them. All human societies do this, and a child growing up into adulthood would be lost without it. But if either in our educational or our general social thinking we start in this way, rather than fashioning doctrines *in vacuo*, that does not make philosophical analysis and argument less relevant. A decision that certain traditional teaching no longer fits the social situation, as in the case of Erikson's Sioux children, may well come from direct social and psychological observation, but in the more frequent case in which we have to distinguish a value of continuing importance from an outmoded form of expression this kind of thinking is very useful. It is useful not because it gives practical answers, but because it suggests approaches that will help us to find the practical answers we should personally prefer. We shall see one example of this when we come to discuss the idea of a liberal education in our present technologically conscious society. We shall have to note the historical changes since the concept was first discussed, and then to disentangle any root idea that we think of permanent value from what may be deemed to be the changing historical accidents of the social settings. This is not an exercise that a philosopher would recognize as rigorous philosophy, but it is a way of going about the tackling of a present-day problem that owes its virtue to the methods of social philosophy. When we have got that far, however, we shall still have to make up our own minds as to the kind of society and environment we want: whether we should prefer cheaper electricity with pylons over beautiful stretches of the South Downs, or the South Downs unspoiled by pylons and dearer electricity; whether we prefer more capital to be invested in school building and less in roadmaking, or vice versa.

The habit of analysing the terms we use is reinforced by familiarity with studies in social philosophy. We have already seen the importance of understanding the difference between the descriptive and the prescriptive use of language, in our discussion as to the bearing on education of statements like "all men are equal." Not less important is the understanding of different "levels" of discourse. At what "level," for instance, are we now prepared to advocate the teaching of national patriotism in our schools?

We are driven to ask this question because we are aware of changes in human society. For nation states to act without regard to the interests of other nation states is now very much more dangerous to us all than it used to be. At the same time, modern communications and many other factors are bringing peoples of different countries much closer together than they have been in the past. In short, our notion of what is our society is widening. It is not so simply to be limited by the boundaries of our particular nation state. This drives us to analyse the idea of patriotism a little. Why have we wanted children to be "patriotic?" What we meant basically was that they should grow up respecting the society into which they had been born, desirous of its good, and ready to defend it. The level at which this was most commonly expressed was readiness to fight for it. But it is precisely the too great readiness of people everywhere to fight for their nation states that menaces the society in which we now live. So we are driven to modify our conception of a desirable patriotism at the surface level, to get down to its underlying justifiable idea, and to redefine that in terms of the changed human society we now live in. This is what we mean when we say that a sense of world citizenship is incompatible only with a superficial, and now dangerous, notion of loyalty to our own country, but that basically it is not only compatible with it but indispensable to it. Once again, this will not give an automatic answer to either political or educational questions—whether, for instance, this country should try to have an independent nuclear deterrent, or whether we should send our own children (if we live in a capital where such a choice is open to us) to an international or a national school. It does indicate movement in certain directions—in the direction of more attention to world history, for instance. But its chief function is to indicate the right kind of approach to thinking about a problem.

This is especially important in a period, like our own, of very rapid social change. Just as in technical education it is foolish to teach mere skills and processes that may be outmoded when a boy gets into a factory, and much more sensible to teach the underlying ideas and to form the habit of applying them, so we need to help the young to think about fundamental values, distinguishing the value from the form in which it is expressed, so that they will not be defeated by a mere change of circumstances or social framework. It goes without saying that in times of rapid educational change, related to the changes in society, this is especially important. It does not mean that we have to turn all our teachers in training, let alone all our citizens, into philosophers. It does mean that, in the modest degree I have indicated, our approach to thinking about educational and social problems should be philosophical.

V

COMPARATIVE

Our disarray in the face of values is not due only to the speed of change in our own culture. It is due almost as much to the discovery, through better acquaintance with other cultures, that what we had taken for certainties were relative rather than universal. This, let it be emphasized is a good thing, not a bad; it makes for comprehension and for tolerance and frees us as hardly anything else could to make our own future with more reasonableness. But it has produced a short-run effect of shock, and in the case of peoples with less established strength than the cultures of the western countries the shock may even have been temporarily paralysing. It is the anthropologists even more than the comparative sociologists of developed cultures that have been responsible for this shock. It is no wonder that the anthropologist Clyde Kluckhohn said, "The matter of values is certainly the prime intellectual issue of the present day."[1] In so far as every society endeavours to perpetuate its social norms through the education it gives its young this is very much an educational question, too. From one point of view comparative education is a branch of anthropology and comparative sociology.

The decisive moment in this turn of events came with the publication in 1935 of Ruth Benedict's famous book *Patterns of Culture*.[2] In this book Dr. Benedict surveyed the social attitudes of three different peoples: the Pueblo Indians of

[1] *Culture and Behaviour*, p. 286 (Free Press of Glencoe, 1962).
[2] Houghton, Mifflin (Boston); Routledge (London).

New Mexico, the inhabitants of Dobu, an island off eastern
New Guinea, and the Kwakiutl Indians of Vancouver Island.
She was less concerned to detail the structure of society
among these different peoples than to show how the totality
of their social life expressed very different values. The
different facets of their life, however surprising when taken
separately, made sense when seen in totality. But what was
"good" in one society was clearly not "good" in another.
And what each society taught its young people to believe to be
good was different.

Now this was a highly intelligent and immensely civilizing
book. One can still reread it with great benefit. To make people see that their particular social norms were not the only
possible good norms, and that other societies had norms that
seemed to work for them just as satisfactorily, was to make a
great contribution to our enlightenment. But did this mean as
Bertrand Russell once quizzically phrased it, that "it seems that
sin is geographical?"[1] In the very last sentence of her book
(where perhaps a writer may be forgiven for making the
main point with a touch of rhetorical emphasis) she used a
phrase for which she has been taken to task. She said, referring
to the consequences of a recognition of cultural relativity:
"We shall arrive then at a more realistic social faith, accepting
as ground of hope and as new bases for tolerance the co-
existing and equally valid patterns of life which mankind has
created for itself from the raw materials of existence." It is
that "equally valid" that has been challenged; and, one must
admit, rightly.

Dr. Benedict's book remains, however, the most influential
general statement of a view of values that the work of a number of anthropologists was reinforcing. What is important to
remember is that she was indeed not calling for a single world
culture, or anything like it, but for a comprehensive under-

[1] *Sceptical Essays*, Introduction (W. W. Norton, 1928).

standing of many cultures, which is a different thing. Yet you cannot understand very different systems of values without at least modifying your sureness that yours alone is right. And even though you recognize the interconnectedness of different features of any one culture (that every upper has a lower and every right a left, as Dr. Benedict put it) you open yourself to influences from outside your own culture. This is true of ideas of education as well as more generally. In comparison is often the beginning not only of tolerance but of wisdom.

Now comparisons of this kind are by no means new, although the work of the anthropologists has reinforced them. Indeed one comparison is classic. We have all been brought up to compare and contrast the values of ancient Athenian and Spartan society, and to compare and contrast their methods of education. There could hardly be a clearer example of the impossibility of separating social from educational values. These two remain the prototypes of education in the free and in the police state.

But who indeed would say that they were equally valid? Clyde Kluckhohn is undoubtedly right in saying[1] that the relativism of Dr. Benedict overlooked two things: that men are men and have certain needs and traits in common however varied their social arrangements; and that some social arrangements and attitudes may reasonably be said to be better to live with than others. This of course does not mean simply for us, who have been conditioned to a particular culture. It means that if you wished well to a new-born baby, so far not culturally conditioned at all, you would choose for him some societies rather than others: a society in which there was general freedom of expression rather than a police state, a society which did not have slavery rather than one that did.

The over-emphasis on cultural relativism has arisen because the temptations to mere dismissal of another culture pattern

[1] *Culture and Behaviour* essays 16 and 17.

are so great. The relativists have been rightly anxious to insist that we must judge a given feature of a culture as part of a totality, not in isolation, and it is relevant to note that Dr. Toulmin has a section in his book on *The Limited Scope of Comparisons between Social Practices*.[1] He says that it is rather unreal to ask whether it is better to have one wife, like Christians, or four wives, as is permitted to Mohammedans. The institution of marriage, in its relations to parenthood, property and so on, is so complex in each kind of society that one must generalize the question somewhat and ask whether Christian marriage or Muslim marriage is the better practice, or even perhaps ask whether the Christian or the Muslim way of life is the better. This is perhaps a little overdrawn: one might reasonably discuss whether a Muslim with four wives (within his Islamic society) is likely, other things being equal, to find more or less satisfaction in marriage than a Christian (within Christian society) with one (though no Benthamite calculus would ever provide a quantitative answer). And one would have to ask about the wives' satisfaction, too. But the warning is salutary.

It is very necessary to heed it when we make comparisons between education in different cultures. One must first understand what are the different social expectations of the schools in the two countries. The American mother who sent her children to a French school while they were temporarily living in France was very puzzled that in the French schools there was apparently none of the familiar American emphasis on "adjustment to the group." When she reflected, she realized that the French school had not had to bear the historic responsibility of the American school to help form into one community children of immigrants from almost every country of the earth. It does not follow that the French schools are bad because they do not have this constant emphasis. It

[1] op. cit., Chapter II.6.

does not follow that American schools promote mere conformism because they do have it. It would be reasonable—so long as one's generalizations were carefully modulated—to point out that the hierarchies of values expressed in American and French society are perceptibly different: that in French society intellectual disagreements are tolerated to the point where to the outsider there seems a danger of breakdown of necessary co-operation, whereas in the United States it is more difficult for the argumentative intellectual to win standing, since he is a figure of suspicion rather than of admiration. Then one might reasonably go on to discuss how far the education in these two countries strengthens the preferences of the respective societies, or modifies them. What is wrong is not to make comparisons—they may be most stimulating and salutary—but to make them without realizing that the values of the schools are closely related to, and commonly expressive of, the values of the society.

If these cautions are heeded, however, comparisons between the educational systems and methods of different countries can be most useful. Some of these comparisons may be statistical, and some may relate to more subtle things. Matthew Arnold used to complain that in our thinking about education we were much too insular in this country, and he tried to explain that with all our insular pride we were behind both France and Prussia in public provision for education. We have become more sensitive to these comparisons in recent years, especially when they appeal to our sporting instincts by being presented in the form of a League table.

One reasonably fair initial comparison is to note how much of the gross national product each year the people of a country spend on education. When the Crowther Committee reported they found that allowing for changes in the value of money we had been spending hardly more than before the war, and that we were not as high in the League table as we ought to be. Since then we have done better. We may be a little behind the United States and the Soviet Union, but the only country in western Europe with which we might fear comparison is Sweden. Before the Robbins Committee reported it was felt that we were very far down the League table in the proportion of each age-group in our population that went to the university. We probably still are, but certain compensating factors emerged from the more detailed analysis given in the Robbins Report.

It is fair to look not only at the figures for entrants to the university but at figures for those who complete their course successfully. If this is done we emerge with rather more credit. But what is a "university?" The term as used in the United States obviously covers institutions that do work of a level that in this country is often done in other institutions of higher education. The fair comparisons are for entrants to full-time higher education as a whole and for those who successfully complete such courses. But again, what is "full-time?" An American college student working his way through and spending several hours a day in wage-earning employment ranks as a full-time student. An English young man working in employment who spends virtually every evening in academic study ranks as a part-time student. These are some of the now familiar pitfalls of international comparisons.

The percentage of the age-group entering full-time higher education in Great Britain in 1958–9 was 7·7, comparing with 9 in France, 12 in Sweden, 30 in U.S.A. and 5 in the Soviet Union. If one refers to all methods of study, part-time as well as full-time, the percentage for Great Britain is 12·5, for France 9, for Sweden 13, for the United States 35, for the Soviet Union 10. The percentage of the age-group completing higher education in 1961–2 was 9·7 in Great Britain (5·2 for courses of degree level), 5 (and 3 for degree level) in France, 7 (and 6) in Sweden, 17 in U.S.A. (with comparison too difficult at degree level) and 7 in the Soviet Union. Wastage is much higher in other countries than in Great Britain, as is obvious from these figures for those who enter and complete respectively.[1]

Again the ratio of full-time members of university staff to full-time university students is more favourable in this country than in any other (1 : 8 in Great Britain, 1 : 30, 12, 13, and 12 in France, Sweden, U.S.A., and U.S.S.R. respectively). This is one reason for the relatively low wastage, and a necessary condition of it. It also goes with the fact that the university course in Great Britain is shorter than in most countries, normally being of three years in England and Wales and of four in Scotland (where entrance to the university is at an earlier age).[1]

But the Robbins Report, if it did something to allay the worst fears about the relative position of this country at present, sounded a serious note of alarm about plans for expansion, where a number of other countries were being far more ambitious than we were. It said—

> The conclusion is plain: the comparison of numbers likely to qualify is no longer favourable, and the disparity in the numbers entering higher education is even wider than it is today. Both in general cultural standards and in competitive intellectual power, vigorous action is needed to avert the danger of a serious relative decline in this country's standing.

It is certainly true that the broad acceptance of the proposals of the Robbins Report for the expansion of higher education was due not only to its argument that we were doing less than we ought to do, but to its demonstration that we were doing and planning to do less than some other countries with which comparison might reasonably be made. The Report was right to point out the misleading nature of unsophisticated international comparisons, but it is to be noted that

[1] *See* Ch. V of the Robbins Report, and relevant Appendices.

it did not renounce the method. On the contrary, having taken all possible precautions as to the meaning of the statistics, it used them as an important element in policy consideration.

The path of the comparative statistician in education is at present indeed a hard one. This is very evident from the work of Professor Edding who, among other labours, was responsible for the statistical part of the paper *Targets for Europe in Education* presented to a conference called by the Organization for Economic Co-operation and Development in Washington in 1961.[1] How does one make valid comparisons between school systems that have different ages of entry, different age-breaks, different kinds of school, different Departments of Government to answer to (with different degrees of central and local expenditure), and enjoying services that are sometimes classed with education and sometimes with health or other categories? This apart from theoretical conundrums, such as whether one should include under the cost of education beyond the compulsory minimum period "opportunity costs" (i.e. the earnings foregone because paid employment was not preferred to continued education). But yet again significant data emerged, perhaps the most interesting being the conclusion that, on the assumption of an economic growth rather less than in previous years, if the countries of western Europe would be content with an increase of expenditure on other goods and services of 58·7 per cent instead of 60 per cent, they could roughly double their expenditure on education by 1970 as compared with 1957. Who would have supposed that the target of doubling our expenditure on education by 1970 could be so easily attainable?

Statistics, or even mere rough estimates of orders of magnitude, will sometimes prompt questions even though they may not answer them. In most European countries there is

[1] Ingvar Svenillson, with the collaboration of Friedrich Edding and Lionel Elvin (O.E.C.D., 1962).

plenty of evidence of increasing demand for higher education, and this is obviously related to the increase in the number of young people staying in formal education beyond the age of fifteen or sixteen. In France they speak of l'*explosion scolaire*; it has necessitated plans for the vast expansion of higher education. Now in the German Federal Republic the visitor finds that there are more educationists than elsewhere who assure him that there is nothing like so great a demand. Working-class people, it is said, want their television sets and their cars, but few of them are really interested in going to the university. Now if this is true some interesting questions arise as to the possible reasons. Is it that the *gymnasium* is not being opened to the sons and daughters of the non-professional classes as much as the *lycée* in France and the grammar school in England? Are there deeper reasons in social psychology for the alleged contentment of the children of working-class parents with their comparatively uneducated lot? Are there reasons for the greater gap than elsewhere between the application rate for higher education and the rate of growth of qualified possible applicants? Or are the German university people who make such statements conservative-minded educationists just deceiving themselves? Is Germany, which has thriven in the past on a highly educated and professionally trained *élite* supported by a mass of workers well trained up to the limits of the technician, perhaps living on its capital in trained manpower? Will the pattern that served it well in the past continue to be adequate in the economic future? Most Germans, looking only inward, would not have much cause to put these questions to themselves. If they look at other comparable countries of western Europe, without mentioning the Soviet Union and the United States, they might indeed wonder whether they are doing enough. It is only when one looks at oneself critically in relation to others that one ceases to believe that one is the only man in the regiment in step.

If the countries of western Europe decide that a considerable expansion of higher education is necessary then they will have increasingly to draw on the children of families that cannot contribute much to the cost of it. This means that there must be much more liberal provision of financial aid to students (either directly or in terms of wages earned through part-time work) and there must also be increased provision of low-cost accommodation. The Americans have now a considerable volume of direct student aid but they have also a long tradition of "working through college." If we in this country placed our main emphasis on working while at college, either the degree course would have to take longer or standards would have to fall. Already tutors have expressed doubts about the increase in the habit of taking vacation jobs: this has clearly extended since a generation ago.

It is difficult to get reliable figures for the financial aid given to students in countries of western Europe.[1] Apart from the Soviet Union none of the countries visited by the Robbins Committee makes provision from public funds for assisting as high a proportion of students as does Great Britain, and in no country is the average sum paid per student assisted so high (not even in the United States). It would seem to be certain that unless their students are in large numbers to exist in misery (and therefore in large numbers to refuse to take up places) the countries of western Europe must do much more in this respect. They are beginning to do so.

The same is true for low-cost accommodation. Traditionally the universities of continental Europe have not been residential. In recent years they have been looking with interest at British and American practice. The *Studentenheim* is

---

[1] A working paper on this subject was presented to the Conference (1964) of the Rectors and Vice-Chancellors of European Universities. As author of the first draft I was able to gather some information through a questionnaire but it was sadly inadequate.

becoming a familiar idea in Germany, and the recent experiment of a residential section (for French students) of the University of Paris just outside the city has met with great approval. Here again international comparison has helped to promote right action.

In summary one may say that the main groups of countries in the world are moving into areas where, for each group, similar problems are encountered. The great problem for the countries with underdeveloped educational systems is to move towards universal primary education while expanding secondary education without waiting for this to be completed, and at the same time to establish their own first independent institutions of higher education. The problem for the countries of western Europe is to universalize secondary education over a reasonably full course and to open up higher education beyond the professional classes. The problem of the United States is both to cope with a still increasing demand for higher education and to plan a reasonable relationship among the variety of institutions, as the State of California is trying to do. There is enough similarity of problems within these main groups, and even to some extent across the groups, to make much cross-fertilization of ideas possible, so long as the precautions we have emphasized are taken in making the comparisons.

When one comes to comparisons of the social purposes and values of education one has of course a different kettle of criteria. Can one say that there are any perennial or universal purposes of education before one gets lost in the differences in different societies? I think one may, and I know of no book in which they are more simply expressed than in an account of his education given by an African who later became an American citizen.[1] He describes his bush education and says that it had three purposes: to give him the knowledge he

[1] PRINCE MODUPE, *I was a Savage* (Museum Press, 1958).

needed (whether of hunting or of the medical properties of certain plants), to initiate him into the wisdom of the elders so that he might understand the traditions and ways of the tribe, and to feel his own nature in unity with the Nature around him. This does not allow for change, perhaps. The African was born into a static society, but with that qualification he had the essentials. In our terms this might read: to give knowledge necessary for living, to prepare for responsible participation in society, to awaken a sense of Man in the Universe. We do not need to add "to become civilized." Maybe this African was brought up as a "savage," but his basis was truly given in his education, and civilization does not require anything different, but only these things brought to a finer quality.

In another place[1] I have recalled that I had no sooner read this book than I picked up the autobiography of a former education officer. He complained bitterly (whether justly or not to his school I cannot say) that on the day he left school he had no skill that would enable him to earn a living, no sense of responsibility to the society he was now to enter, and belief neither in himself nor in a God. The comment is pretty obvious: he had not been educated, and in precisely the three basic things in which the "savage" had. The conditions were different, but the needs to which both writers referred were perennial and universal.

But how far can we sharpen our sense of what is important, and is perhaps neglected in the education of a particular society, by comparison with education in a different one? Here it is difficult not to be impressionistic and personal. Certainly, any one who has seen something of different countries will realize how deep in social patterns some educational differences lie. To some extent in the secondary schools (certainly

[1] In my essay in *The Humanist Frame*, ed. by Sir Julian Huxley (Allen and Unwin, 1961).

in the sixth form in England), and very much in the universities, the assumption between teacher and students is of a
republic, not a monarchy of discourse. But those who have
taught students from Asian and Middle Eastern countries
know how hard it is to break down the barrier of politeness
that exalts the *guru* too much above the disciple. As my former
colleague in UNESCO, Dr. W. D. Wall, has observed, this
is part of the whole pattern of behaviour expected of the
superior and the inferior in a relationship in an eastern country.
The disciple-student is there humbly to learn from the *guru*-
teacher. The teacher, too, has his obligations: to teach the
truth as he understands it and to treat the disciple with personal
helpfulness. But the student knows that his first obligation
is to give pleasure and satisfaction to his teacher. He must
divine what the teacher wishes him to say, and then say it.
The reply, quite possible from an undergraduate in an English
or an American university, "but surely that is not so" or even
"but that's nonsense," would be an intolerable breach of good
manners. Here, I think, the westerner would stand firm.
Good manners and disagreement, even cheerfully blunt disagreement, are compatible; and education in its higher levels
is impossible without it.

This difficulty is allied to the difficulty of getting a student
to think for himself if his whole experience has been one of
learning by rote. Can you really be said to have read if you
have only memorized the words and have not reflected on
them so that you have come to a conclusion that you have
made your own? The former may do in a static society, if it
is only a question of memorizing the wisdom of the elders.
It will not do at all in a modern society in which both scientifically and socially we have to think for ourselves and be
capable of breaking through the traditional. One may opt
for the static. But it is of no use to suppose that one can learn
science as one memorizes verses from the Koran. If one wants

a modern society one must want its distinctive values also and use its distinctive methods.

Unfortunately, as Dr. Benedict said, every upper implies a lower and every right a left. English or American visitors to schools in the Soviet Union must have been struck by the earnestness to learn that one finds there. The young are not distracted by all the things that tend to distract a western boy and girl in surrounding society. The teacher does not have to compete with shrieking commercial hoardings, "comics," and all the vulgarities that are meant to appeal to the child's or the teen-ager's pocket. The atmosphere is almost Victorian (I had strangely mixed feelings when I was told by one school librarian that the book most often taken out was *Quentin Durward*—I could not imagine that in England or America). But what does this go with? A general censorship in literature and an equally Victorian acceptance of dogma. The fact that the dogma comes from Marx rather than Moses, from Karl rather than Calvin, is incidental. Is it possible to have freedom to think critically about even the most cherished dogmas of society without conceding a freedom that may be misused at the expense of the young? One would like to think it was. Neither western capitalism nor monolithic communism has found the answer. Meanwhile it does neither harm to have a good steady look at the other.

So far comparative education has hesitated to be explicitly comparative. It has largely been a matter of studies of education in other countries. One can understand the scruples. They are a little like the scruples of the sociologists and the philosophers that we have already seen. But we need more statistical comparisons, and more academically disciplined comparisons between the educational values of different societies. If undertaken with due scholarly scruples and with understanding such comparison could be immensely illuminating.

Comparative education is as important a determinant of our basic disciplined thinking about education and society as any of the three other disciplines we have considered in this first Part. It does over space what historical study does over time. Both are indispensable for widening our experience and helping us to see our own problems in proper perspective.

VI

FROM STUDIES TO POLICIES

WE have now considered some of the studies, sociological, psychological, philosophical, and comparative, that contribute to our thinking about education and contemporary society. But what is the nature of their relevance when you have to face particular problems or work out specific policies? How much use are they? This is a question that often perplexes teachers in training, who are expected to follow courses labelled "Education" and wonder how they bear on what they will do in the classroom or on public educational policy. Before coming on to discuss some of our contemporary problems I should like, therefore, to explain the nature of the connexion between the two parts of this book.

If those who taught the relevant theoretical disciplines were all in agreement with one another (and of course they are not) it would not follow that they would be agreed as to educational policy. As we have noted, the philosophers have said that they must not be relied on for solutions to practical problems. The psychologists and sociologists do not impose quite so stern a self-denying ordinance, but they too would point out that research and policy-making are not the same thing. The comparative educationist would issue a warning of his own special kind: that direct policy conclusions, read over from one social context to a different one, would be dangerous. Then, it may be asked, why bother with these studies at all?

One obvious point may be made first. The policy maker

has to take into account factors that the research worker rightly ignores (the state of public opinion, for instance). But this does not mean that the results of research are not a necessary element in good policy thinking. Research studies provide data without which policy-making may go very wrong. But one may say more. Research studies, and theoretical work generally, may give a general direction to policy thinking. Negatively, they may show that common arguments against a proposed policy are without adequate foundation (if the work of Professor Husén in Sweden continues to show that abler children do not suffer seriously from being in a common school up to the age of, say, fifteen or sixteen, that will lead to a reconsideration of one of the main arguments against the Swedish school reform). Positively, they may persuade us to change our practice (the increasing understanding that young children learn very largely through play has meant that we build infant schools differently from the horrors of the last century). But the main point about these studies is not that they point to exact practical answers. It is that they affect the level of our thinking.

Now this is not an easy matter to explain, though we are in fact quite familiar with the idea. If, for instance, in an examination in a teachers training college or in a university department of education there were a question about the comprehensive school, we should not mark the answers in accordance with whether they were for or against it. We should mark in accordance with the level at which the discussion was carried on. Similarly in matters of public educational policy. Decisions are made, and rightly, for reasons that go beyond research findings; but they should not be made in ignorance of them, and they should be made at a good level of understanding. If, for instance, we are opposed to selection for different kinds of secondary school at the age of eleven it is important that we should not, except perhaps as a kind of shorthand, talk of "abolishing the eleven plus." We should understand the difference between condemning a selection at that age and condemning the tests used. We could take the view that the selection is wrong and that the tests used (the decision to select having been made) are good. We should understand that whatever system of secondary education we have it is desirable to know as much as tests can tell us about the abilities of different children. We should understand that in any secondary school system a measure of streaming is likely at some stage or other, and that this must have a proper basis. In other words, the level of the discussion, irrespective of whether the decision goes one way or another, is of very great importance. In some circumstances indeed we might prefer to see an intelligent and sensitive trial given to the policy we favoured less, rather than to witness a stupid attempt to carry out the policy we preferred.

What are some of the factors, over and above research findings, that cause a decision of public educational policy to be made in one direction rather than another? One I have already mentioned, the state of public opinion. In the next section we shall be considering the problem of the structure of secondary education. Now, as we have already seen, there are research findings of great significance, coming from the sociologists and social psychologists, that we must take into account. We know that education is a determinant of social class, and equally we realize more strongly than we did that social class is a determinant of educability. If we would like our society to differentiate us less into classes or social groups than it does now, here is a value judgement, and the recent sociological work to which we have referred will strengthen our resolve to have a structure of secondary education that does not accentuate these social divisions. Other things being reasonably equal, we should favour a less selectively differential structure than we have at present. But not every one does feel this way.

And some no doubt feel it, but not strongly enough for them to agree to throwing away (as they see it) the educational advantages that a differential structure is thought to entail. What is really important is to get the discussion on to the right level: to know what the reasonably sure findings of research are, to know where these must be regarded as still tentative, and then to know when, whatever the findings, we are making a value judgement as to the kind of society we should prefer.

In a good number of local education authority areas there is now discussion of changes in the secondary school structure. A wise education officer will wish to carry with him not only his education committee and the general public, but the teachers in the authority's schools. Some are now carefully and systematically initiating discussions among the teachers, and putting the evidence before them as fairly as they can. The result could be that the education officer realized that he could not carry through with their assent the particular changes he himself would favour; and in that case he might be right to go as far as he could with their support rather than to try to get an imposed solution of the kind he favoured.

Again, in matters of public education policy, we never start with a blank sheet. Physically, we have schools already built and in use, and built according to particular assumptions as to the kind of structure we need. If we decide, influenced by research findings, that a different structure would be better, we have to decide also how far an adaptation of existing buildings is possible to enable us to change the structure as we desire. The answer will be different in different places.

Now all this does not mean that theoretical studies are simply an interesting exercise and nothing to do with practical work. When people get into this frame of mind something is very wrong. I once asked a group of students in a training college how they would react if confronted by a boy who was being an intolerable nuisance in a class in which they were doing their practice teaching. Would they consider what treatment rather than what punishment he should have, reflecting that it was no doubt their fault, or his home's, or society's, that he was behaving so anti-socially? Or would they say, "Stop it, you?" Their answer, I am afraid, was that the first reaction was what they were taught in college was the right one—but the second reaction was the one they would certainly use. I had to point out that if there was such a gap between theory and practice something must be wrong either with the theory or with the practice. Our integrity could not tolerate so wide a gap. As we discussed the problem certain rather better distinctions came out, such as that between the immediate situation in which the teacher's control had to be maintained and the longer-term policy (assuming that in an actual post they would be longer with the class) in which the first group of considerations would come much more into play. What mattered was not that they should say one reaction was right and the other wrong, but that they should think it out at a proper level.

One prerequisite for this is a reasonable skill in analysing the terms and concepts we use. The connexion between philosophy and educational decision-making seems less immediate than that with sociology and psychology. But it is just here that it is useful. Take, for instance, the word "ought." Let me recall the two uses of this word, the categorical and the hypothetical. "We ought to make education more democratic" is one kind of statement. "If we want to make our education more democratic we ought to have more comprehensive schools" is a statement of a different kind. The first "ought" expresses a value judgement. The second "ought" is consequential merely: that is to say, the second statement assumes the value judgement as accepted and then indicates an alleged consequence of accepting it. In the remaining part of this book I shall be assuming that on the whole we want a society of a certain kind in this country and my "oughts" will be mostly consequential. Two kinds of objection will be in order. Either that my assumptions are wrong or that the consequences do not in fact follow. I should add, of course, that if I do make certain assumptions as to the kind of society we should want I am bound to some extent to have made a less explicit assumption that this is the kind of society I should want, hoping others will agree with me; and there will be value judgements there.

What I am maintaining, however, is that two things must be borne in mind, though it is not easy to keep them both properly in mind at the same time. The first is that our practice must be consonant with research and theory, and secondly that it cannot follow from research and theory in a one to one logical sequence, because in practice other things also have to be taken into account. In what follows I shall not attempt a systematic justification of the values I assume, though I shall commend them; and I emphasize that those who may share them might still come to different policy conclusions.

There are many problems in educational policy that we might take for such discussion. I shall select only a few of the more important areas. If we are to take account of the sociological and psychological work we have just reviewed, then, as I have already indicated, a crucial question is that of our educational structure. This happens also to be an area in which we cannot avoid some sort of reconciliation of claims, of the kind that the philosophers have warned us is especially difficult; the claim of the abler children to benefit from selectively differentiated education, and the claim that all children should be educated as members of the same society. As a kind of extended footnote to this I should like to raise the question as to what we mean by *élites* in our society.

I should then like to move on to a discussion of the kind of values that we should like education to encourage in future members of our society. Here we shall be concerned less with policies than with what might be called policy attitudes. How do we rate intellectual values in our society? How are we to promote the values of a liberal education in a techno-logical age? What should be the role of the schools in pro-moting moral values, and how do these relate to the moral values of surrounding society? And how far ought the schools to give a sense of community to our future citizens?

The terms in which these questions have to be answered are changing, as compared for instance with only thirty or forty years ago. To discuss that we need to have at the back of our minds what sociological, psychological and comparative studies can tell us; and also, although the brief discussions that follow are certainly not "philosophy" they do, I trust, show something of the habit of mind that asks questions of concepts and distinguishes values from the mere forms in which they may have been expressed.

But how do we go about such discussions?

Logically, no doubt, we should first think out what kind of society we want and then we should devise a system of education that would prepare each new generation to take its place in it. Only so, as Plato understood, can we be certain that a good society will endure. Yet this logic, so persuasive if you are writing a Utopia, is far too abstract. After all we live in an actual society, and we know it fairly well; and our children are already in actual schools. As C. L. Stevenson said of the role of reasoning in refining our sense of values, we start where we are and discuss what modifications we want from where we stand at present. And since this book is about educational problems in our society, and is not a study of modern society as such, I shall assume that we know (or can find out) enough about the society we live in for our present purpose and so come quickly to discussion of our educational problems themselves. I must, however, say just a little about the nature of our society to indicate the framework within which our discussion will go on.

What should we say if we were asked to characterize English society, at least in general terms? We should find ourselves using a number of words, embodying concepts that had real meaning, but needing considerable detailed explanation if they were to describe our society rather than any other. We should also have to admit that not everybody would give the same weight to each of the concepts we invoked. We should say, for instance, that we thought of ourselves as a democracy, and that by itself would be enough to mark us off from societies that were dictatorships. But we are a historically mixed polity and a historically mixed society, and some English people are more ardently democratic than others. We should note that the word democracy originally served to distinguish one form of government from others, such as tyrannies and oligarchies, but has become rather wider in its connotations now. We might be asked if this country was a social democracy. We might question this use of the word, though it has become so general that we should be a little foolish not to ask what those who use it mean and how far this meaning applies to our own society.

When we left static descriptions and asked what the perceptible tendencies of English society were, and asked moreover in which direction the people of this country wanted society to move, we should be on more controversial ground. If, for instance, we said there was a tendency towards a more planned society, we should have to note that some would say: "indeed, yes; we can't expect to muddle through for ever"; while others might say: "we might perhaps think ahead a little more, but we don't want central control over everybody and everything—there's too much of that already." We should have to strike a balance, and we should probably agree that there has been something of a change of emphasis in recent years. Before the last war, if any one used the word planning he felt himself going against the English grain. That is not so now. We are on our guard against monolithic and over-centralized planning, but on the whole we accept the need for more and better planning of our economic and social development.

In very general terms most of us would feel we could say we were a moderately prosperous, democratic and civilized society, relatively speaking at least; and that we wished to move in the direction of a more assured prosperity, a stronger sense of democratic life, and a more widespread sense of civilized values. All of these involve a degree of planning, and we believe that this planned development, though the consequence of directional indications of some force, should result as far as possible from a consensus of opinion after debate in a pluralist society. In particular any rivalries between these aims must be talked out so as to give the best resolution of forces possible in any given set of circumstances (for instance, many people would wish to be assured that democratic extension did not endanger the civilized qualities that may be the achievement of a minority and yet indispensable to a good society as a whole). We should all agree that the maintenance of what is good in our present society, as well as the possibility of its improvement in all these directions, will depend very much on education.

These, it may be said, are generalities, perhaps mere platitudes. They hardly give us a sure guide for the devising of policies. Moreover they presuppose that our social development depends chiefly upon the discussion of ideas. They overlook the fact that there are struggles for power in all societies, and that that is what politics (and, therefore, all the things we are discussing) are ultimately about. I am aware of the force of these objections, though they too might be said to be somewhat confident generalizations. Nevertheless our general concepts give us a starting point. A society whose members talk in these terms is clearly differentiated from those societies where they do not. These concepts mark it also as belonging to a general group of societies, that of itself and its ideological neighbours, however significant the differences within the group may be. Since, as has been said, we are not pursuing an analysis of our society as such, it would seem sensible to leave this discussion of what it is like at this general level, and to allow the necessary qualifications to come out in the study of the educational problems themselves.

On the assumption, then, that we want a society with civilized values, and a reasonably well-planned, prosperous, democratic and pluralist one in particular, we may take up the discussion of some of our educational problems where the interaction between education and society is of especial importance.

PART II · PROBLEMS AND POLICIES

VII

THE DEMOCRATIZATION OF EDUCATION

THE recent sociological and psychological research we have surveyed undoubtedly has policy implications. It will suggest to most people, given the general feelings in our society about affording individuals reasonably equal chances so far as we can, that there is a stronger case for modifications of our educational system in the direction of equality than had been supposed before this work had taken place. There is also a frequently heard argument that the extension of our educational provision, and the opening of higher and specialized branches of it to more young people, is necessary for the development of the economy; and if we had looked also at the work of the economists of education we should have found a good deal of supporting evidence for this argument. The general effect of these two kinds of studies, converging towards a policy attitude, is to favour what in shorthand terms might be called the increasing "democratization" of education.

One can now say that there are these two main acknowledged general reasons for the extension of formal education in modern and would-be modern societies: it is necessary for a technically efficient economy, and it is demanded as a right. The force of these claims is most obvious in the developing low-income countries. But if we choose to think, say, of India and Nigeria in this context we must not forget that England and the United States are developing too. They, and the countries like them, may be more fortunate: they have universal primary education, general secondary education, a well-developed higher education, and good technical education and training. But the pressure is on them too, pressure for more education as a right and as a need of a still further developing economy.

It is not necessary to go into the old argument as to whether the economic need or the idea is primary. If it is said that the economic need is primary it must be recognized that there soon develops an independent pressure for the granting of more education as a right. In some of the low-income countries this pressure is so strong that it is not easy for governments to insist on that degree of secondary and higher education, before there is universal primary education, without which a newly independent country cannot have the trained manpower it needs.

The economic argument by itself would be decisive in favour of the extension of education. But as soon as it is acted upon effects are generated which are more than economic. The educational development of the Soviet Union has been closely geared to the country's economic needs, but the effects are now being felt in a non-economic demand for a greater cultural and intellectual freedom. This general effect is in part due to the fact that the economic argument is itself a general one. Forecasting of the number of persons needed in a series of employments perhaps ten years ahead cannot be exact. Still less can the correlation of these manpower needs with educational provision of a specialist kind. Good general education is a prerequisite for technical education, especially as technological processes now change so quickly; and since also people change their employments in the course of their working lives correlations with educational levels must be general, not precise.

What one may say is that as an economy develops the proportions of the main sections of the total working population change. This is the result of technological improvement, calling for fewer and fewer workers, and more mechanical resources, for each unit of production. If one thinks of the total working population as consisting of five groups, unskilled, semi-skilled and skilled workers and lower and higher managerial staff, then as an economy develops fewer unskilled workers will be needed, rather fewer semi-skilled, and fewer "workers" altogether than other staff. These different levels can be roughly equated with educational levels, and to this extent the manpower demands of the economy on the educational system can be quantified. The SVIMEZ study of the future demands of the Italian economy on the educational system of that country[1] showed that much greater developments in education would be necessary than had been supposed. The recent Report on Higher Education of the State of Kansas showed, on the same kind of reasoning, that considerable extension of higher education would be necessary in that state. This is reason enough for making sure that educational expansion takes place. But at the same time people increasingly want such extension for themselves, as good in its own right; and broad social effects follow this change.

A Marxist might say that just as the Education Act of 1870 in England corresponded to the industrialists' need for workers who were literate, so the Education Act of 1902 met the need for minor managerial employees and members of the professions that did not yet enjoy full professional prestige —schoolteachers, dentists, accountants, bank and insurance employees, and so on. Maybe; but before long the members of

[1] *Trained Manpower Requirements in the Next Fifteen Years* (Associazione per lo sviluppo dell'industria nel Mezzogiorno, Rome, 1960).

these professions were claiming full professional recognition and stepping up their qualifications for entry. Some of the boys and girls at these secondary schools were beginning to enter the ranks of university teachers, lawyers and doctors. In short they were achieving a social standing of their own.

It is these social groups that are now demanding higher education for their children. There is a very common pattern over three generations in England today: grandfather ending his formal education with the elementary school (and perhaps continuing with some adult education classes), father ending with the secondary school (and getting a professional qualification by evening work), son or daughter going to university or training college. Parents and young people believe this last stage to be one that they should be accorded as of right. This is only the form taken in the more advanced countries of a worldwide phenomenon characteristic of this second half of the twentieth century, the belief that education (and more of it) is a right. Of course it is not an absolute but a contingent right. It is contingent on the capacity of a country to bear the costs involved, and it is contingent on the capacity of those who make the demand to show that they are able and willing to profit by such continued education. The first condition need not unduly worry countries with an advanced economy capable of steady expansion, though it should not be forgotten that the expansion of the social services does depend on the state of the economy, since funds do not fall from heaven. The second condition merits further elucidation.

No voice is publicly raised against the principle of the democratiziation of education now. But if it is to become a reality we have to consider what equality of opportunity to qualify for better education amounts to in our present society. It is clear from what research workers have found that there will not be reasonable equality of opportunity to qualify until

ve move nearer to economic and social equality. This is true
f we consider the public sector of education alone. If, as Dr.
Douglas said, we include the private sector in our view (and
ve must if we are thinking of our whole society) "all semblance
of social equality vanishes."

If we believe it to be right to do something about this it
will be in large measure the result of a social, not merely an
educational, conscience. The Newsom Report has already
made it clear that without such remedial social action many of
our schools, and therefore many of our children, will never
have a fair chance. That social conscience and social action
are so linked with education is no novel doctrine—

> To the study of education at the present time in this country,
> in America, in Germany, and in France, there is an evident growth
> of feeling that school problems, though of course in some respects
> a special subject by themselves, are only seen in their true perspect-
> ive when they are regarded as being in necessary and constant
> relation to other forms of social culture. The educational question
> is not a question by itself. It is part of the social question. And
> the social question is at bottom largely an ethical question.

This was said by Sir Michael Sadler as long ago as 1902.[1] The
difference now is that the ethical point is much more widely
conceded, though so far we have not acted adequately upon it.
The steps we have taken towards the Welfare State have made
a difference, but we have been somewhat too complacent about
their extent. Recent studies have made us realize that there is
still a submerged tenth of our people, some would say a
submerged fifth. We had begun to think that we had hardly
any slums now, but recent studies have shaken that view.
There are schools in slum areas of our big cities and there are
many schools in the countryside that lack the most obvious
amenities. It is true, of course, that vigorous social and political
action could put this right within a matter of years. It is also

[1] Quoted by Dr. Brian Holmes in an unpublished thesis.

true that there will always be variations, for individual familie
and schools; the presence or absence of a bathroom is no
always a determinant of values. But we still have with us
as Mrs. Floud has pointed out, the lower educability that in
general goes with unequal economic resources, unequal
cultural opportunities, and a generally low social status.

What can be done about this inequality through educational
policy alone? One of the most important elements in the
problem is our educational structure, by which I mean the
disposition of our different institutional units in relation to one
another, either in chronological sequence or as alternatives for
members of the same age-group. In England we have a
chronological sequence: infant school, junior school, secondary school, with breaks at the ages of seven and eleven. And
at the secondary stage we have parallel institutions for the
same age-group: grammar school, technical school, and
modern school. Put briefly the problem is this: how far
should social considerations and how far should teaching
considerations govern our decision as to the kind of educational
structure we have, and also how far do these two kinds of
consideration run counter to one another? The problem in
relation to the chronological sequence is where to make the
age-breaks. The problem in relation to the varied provision
for the same age-group is how to reconcile the need to promote
a sense of social community with intellectual diversity.

Now this is a question to think out in principle; a policy
based on administrative convenience or parsimony only would
be wrong. But, as I have already briefly noted, a policy cannot
be reasonably put forward that does not take account of
existing resources of buildings and teachers and that does not
use them well, even though their present deployment is
based on a different plan from what might be our ideal. In an
area where the school population may be falling in relation to
the rest of the country we cannot scrap the present structure

of school education and have something quite different that would entail a great new building programme leaving some of the existing schools unused. In contrast, where a new town has to be built an education authority is almost untrammelled by the past and can put into effect the plan it thinks best. For this reason of local diversity alone, and apart from the fact that different local communities may want different school structures (and within reason should be given their head), we must expect variety rather than one system for the whole country.

There is, of course, a certain temptation to use the argument that schools have been built of a certain size, or that staff have been trained and engaged for certain purposes, in defence of a temperamental conservatism. The remedy for this is to notice that other countries do not do things in our way: conceivably in some things they may be on a better track than we are. For instance, in England children must go to school at the age of five. This is earlier than in any other country of Europe and earlier than anywhere in the United States. When a suggestion is made that half-time schooling might be educationally better for the first year it is rather ridiculous to hear progressive voices raised in unreasoning horror. We might be right, and the rest of the world behind us. But this is a natural and legitimate question to raise in view of the different practice everywhere else, and the case has to be argued out. Again, the distribution of time between primary and secondary education has varied from country to country and from time to time in particular countries. There can be a pattern of eight years primary followed by four years secondary education; or of six years primary followed by four compulsory and three more optional secondary years, as with ourselves now (with five compulsory and two voluntary, as we shall have when the minimum leaving age is raised to sixteen); or of a first cycle of three years and a second cycle of three in the same secondary school; or of a junior secondary school for three years separate from the senior secondary school for the next three; or of a continuous school from the age of entry right up to fifteen or sixteen, with either a "modern" school for two years or an academic secondary school for three or four following that. In this country, we have the comprehensive secondary school as well as the tripartite system, many modifications of the latter, and some experimental schemes that are of their own kind, as in Leicestershire. There is no one perfect pattern (not even the present one, whatever it happens to be!). There are choices open to us, and we must think seriously about them. As I have said, we must remember that local circumstances must be taken into account and that we cannot ignore what is on the ground already. But we must also think of principles, and above all of the principle that, in the interest both of the use of our potential ability and of social justice, there must be the greatest attainable equality of opportunity for different children to show what they can do, and to do it. And, as we have seen, this now means doing what we can to make their condition more nearly equal.

We have seen how early in life chances in education become unequal. This is partly in the nature of things: we can hardly legislate to ensure that children have equally loving, cultivated and intelligent parents. It is partly social, and we could do more to see that our poorer areas are brought up to a respectable national minimum of amenity. There is some small scope for early educational action, especially in the provision of nursery schools. The nursery school long ago proved its value, but we still have very few of them. It is very difficult to get more because of the shortage of teachers, a shortage that gets worse the lower down the age-range one goes. But this is the best partial answer to early home inequality that we could give.

In the primary school we have seen how disparity increases between the favoured and the less favoured. There is a lessening of equal chances between the ages of eight and eleven. This is due partly to differences in home and neighbourhood background, but it is enhanced by the differences between primary schools. There will always be some schools that are better than others, whatever one understands by better. But there is now a prestige among primary schools in terms of their success in getting children through the "eleven plus." Parents who are serious about the education of their children, and have the social confidence to push a little in their favour, try to get them into these primary schools rather than into those with poor eleven plus records. These differences are then accentuated by streaming in many primary schools, and although less than half of the primary schools are large enough to stream, streaming is both very common and, as Dr. Douglas pointed out, more rigid than people suppose. And that streaming is often justified by the teachers by the need to get as many of the brighter children through the eleven plus as possible. We have made things difficult for ourselves with our zeal for premature selection!

We are now being increasingly convinced that in spite of the excellence of the tests we use we cannot select for different kinds of secondary school at eleven with reasonable exactness and justice. There is always a considerable group round the borderline who are wrongly placed as judged by their subsequent achievement. And the selection though not absolutely final, is apt in most cases to prove so. Selection for the secondary grammar school carries great prestige, and non-selection the opposite. The attempt to persuade parents that this is not an examination but a placing in the best interests of the children has broken down. It never was a very honest claim given social realities. At best it was an honest hope.

Whatever refinements may have been absent from this or

that study, the evidence of the failure of this selection at eleven is now conclusive. When the Croydon authority put forward its plan for the reorganization of secondary education it did so on the basis of three careful reports as to how its selection system had worked. It found that a considerable proportion of the non-selected had done better in subsequent school achievement than a considerable proportion of the selected. Authority after authority is now coming to the same conclusion. When the sense of injustice (as illustrated by the bitterness, reported by Dr. Douglas, of so many of the mothers of the rejected children) is added to the failure—in spite of great technical skill—of this selection to do its job, there is only one possible conclusion: it must end. It has been a very bad mistake.

Going to a school with a status higher or lower than that of others is not simply a matter of where you take your lessons. It largely governs your choice of friends. If you go to a grammar school, or alternatively to a secondary modern school, you move in a different *milieu*, even if you go to one and your brother or sister goes to the other. In the grammar school the picture of the future is different: your eyes are set on the professions or executive posts. If you are in the modern school you know that barring great efforts and some good fortune such a status is denied to you. Fortunately human nature is often resilient and many of these youngsters have their own confidence and are not too depressed by the label that seems to have been set upon them. But the label is there. The heads and the staffs of the modern schools sometimes do wonders, but they have to fight a needlessly uphill battle. It is wrong that the head of such a school should have to say to the parents of his incoming group of boys and girls, "I know I am speaking to disappointed parents," and then work on uphill from there. There will always be boys and girls who do not do well at school, and parents who will be disappointed. We

annot abolish that if we "abolish the eleven plus." The point
s that we now structure and institutionalize the disappointment.

Any reasonably sensitive person can feel this division now in
English life. This sense of separation over the minor inter-
changes and pleasantnesses of life does not happen in the
United States, and the English visitor to that country is struck
by the difference. There is indeed consciousness of status in
America, and it is often tied too much to income; but there is
a kind of free and easy democracy of behaviour (without the
pulling oneself in that one feels in England) that in this respect
makes American society a richer and more cheerful one. The
barriers that one feels in England, of dress, of accent, of style of
life, are not there all the time.

The explanation is in part at least that almost all
Americans go to the common school. In this country now,
over and above our division between the publicly maintained
and the private schools, we freeze ourselves into separate
groups at eleven.

There is an increasing feeling that the "eleven plus" is on its
way out now. But there is no general agreement as to what
should take its place. Local circumstances, as has been said,
will vary enough to make any insistence on some single overall
pattern foolish, but it is worth discussing in what direction the
important educational and social considerations point. What,
for instance, is to be said for various ages at which there should
be a change of school?

A change of school may be disturbing to a child, or it may
be stimulating. If he is the only one to move it may well be
disturbing. If he is one of a whole group moving to the
adventure of a new stage in life it may be stimulating. But
why was the age of eleven chosen after the last war? If we were
starting with a clean sheet should we say that eleven marked
a natural break between two periods of life? The Hadow

Report of 1926 tried to argue this, but the argument rested chiefly on an unsupported metaphor about blood coursing faster through the veins at this age (by which they presumably meant that boys were beginning to look at girls—a somewhat inadequate treatment of the onset of adolescence). The old elementary school that ran on to thirteen or fourteen knew nothing of such a break. Standard five was one above standard four and one below standard six, that's all. There was just a steady gradation up the school. The concept of adolescence is too vague to permit of a precise indication and the physical and emotional signs of it are spread over a fairly large period in a group of boys and girls. The explanation for the choice of eleven really goes back to the "Hadow" reorganization of the thirties and the reasons were largely historical and administrative. Educational opinion was in favour then and there was no psychological argument against eleven. No one now believes there is in fact any particular argument for it either.

If selection for different kinds of secondary school at eleven is not satisfactory and the public is becoming so convinced of this that we shall have to make changes, we need to think out what we would most desire in any alternative arrangements. Because any chosen alternative will represent a compromise between different desiderata, not all of which are compatible with each other, people who may agree as to what things are desirable may weight them differently and so come out in practice with different policies. But if we can isolate the elements we should wish to see expressed in alternative arrangements that will bring us nearer agreement.

The first need, on which nearly everybody would be agreed now, is to make the selection later (if, that is, there is to be selection at all). The reason for this used to be expressed by saying that although you could test general intelligence quite early, the special aptitudes mostly revealed themselves later. We are less confident now about this distinction between general intelligence and special aptitudes; but this makes it more, not less, doubtful whether tests of general intelligence at eleven give a sure basis for a selection that implies at least general kinds of career. Can you be sure at this age that you can separate out the future technologist from the future technician? It would seem to be very doubtful.

The second need is for selection to become as far as possible self-selection. Why? Such self-selection should of course come after a good deal of consultation and counselling, but ultimately the boy or girl will say, "I want to stay on at school and continue my formal education," or on the contrary, "I've had enough of school and want to get a job." To make this self-selection possible for a large number of young people would be an immense solvent of present frustration and injustice. The apparent wastefulness of the American acceptance of large entries to colleges and universities, with the discharge of up to thirty or forty per cent after the first year, is often defended on the ground that this allows a great number of would-be students to have a chance to show whether they are suitable and, if they are not, to discover this for themselves. In this country we could not afford such a method, but the argument has force. At the school level we should certainly be able to come nearer to self-selection than we now are. A main aim must always be to bring young people to a realistic acceptance of themselves and to a reconciliation of aspiration with ability. But there is a great deal of difference between the use of guidance and the use of something like force as the main way of bringing this about. Anything a society can do to increase the area of consent and assent, and to diminish the feeling that "we" have been put upon by "them" is likely to make for greater harmony and goodwill.

Thirdly, it has been recognized from the early days of the 1944 Act that young people of secondary school age ought to have the benefit of being at schools that enjoy general parity of esteem. This does not mean that a single school will not have a higher reputation, or a lower one, than others; but that there will not be inequality of standing between groups or kinds of school. There was great talk of establishing such parity of esteem with the grammar school for the secondary modern and technical schools. It has not happened, and for reasons that might have been foreseen. By and large the grammar school takes a boy or girl into careers and social groups that do enjoy higher incomes and higher social standing. It is the parents, not the educational pundits, whose instincts have been right about this. If, then, we are not going to get such parity of esteem after differential selection has taken place, there is a stronger case than we had recognized for not differentiating so early and for having children longer in the same kind of school. This is the social complement to the psychological argument for postponing selection.

If the first of these three criteria is chiefly technical, the second and third involve value judgements. But they are not value judgements with which any appreciable number of people would disagree, in themselves. The difficulty comes in weighting them as compared with other criteria that are also important. The most important of these, expressing it in broad terms, is that our concern for the average or academically below average child must on no account lead us to prejudice the emergence as fully qualified people of our abler boys and girls. One can be unjust to the able, as well as to the less able, if they are not encouraged to develop their potential capacities and gifts. And, moreover, although the quality of a civilization is not to be judged by its few outstanding individuals only, nevertheless the progress of a civilization depends very much indeed on its abler groups.

The corollary of this is held to be that you must to some extent educate the abler boys and girls separately from the rest, partly because you can teach them better if they are in a group that can go ahead at its own fast pace, and partly because the effect of their stimulus on each other will be greater if they form a separate group. This, if true, would seem to run counter to our first three desiderata and point to a school structure with earlier differentiation, not later. But there are in reality a number of different things to disentangle in this simple statement of the case that we have had before us so far.

There is no doubt that there is something in this argument, but equally that there are different weights to be attached to it at different ages. This is because the gap between two different children, one of high intellectual age in relation to his chronological age and the other of low, becomes wider, as a matter of mere arithmetic, as they both get older. At five you can teach them together more easily than at fifteen. But then we must formulate our question correctly. We are not really speaking of ease of teaching for the teacher so much as effectiveness of learning for the young, and these are not quite the same things. Learning goes on when the teacher is not formally teaching. We have to establish, not how far it is easier for a teacher to teach an intellectually homogeneous class, but how far the young learn faster and better in such a class. And then again we have to take a fairly long view. There is no doubt that if you are cramming a few pupils to get through an examination in six months' time you (and they) will have a better chance if they are coached separately. But it does not necessarily follow that able children taught in a separate school from eleven to eighteen will have developed their academic abilities further at eighteen than if they had been at the same school with other children for a part or the whole of the time till eighteen. What we can reasonably say is that the case for separate teaching would seem to be stronger as the age goes up. The evidence from Sweden to which I have referred earlier suggests that there is no particular advantage even for the ablest up to the age of fourteen or so, and that there is a great advantage in stimulus from being with the ablest for the next group. If the question is put as to whether keeping everybody together till, say, fifteen would handicap the ablest at all, we can only say that we do not know, either way. My own guess would be that there would be a slight keeping back, but in view of the general pressures we put on our academically abler children I should not mind a slight holding back at this age if it were made up, as I think it would be, by eighteen. What of course must make a difference is not only arrangements between schools but arrangements within schools. There are devices from streaming to "setting" (taking children in different groups according to their ability in different subjects) which may be used to give the fastest their heads within a single school.

The second consideration that may go against the first three we mentioned concerns not the above average but the average and below average children. There is a case for their separate treatment, in their own interest, as well. The Newsom Report says with emphasis that for those young people who have decided that they will leave school as soon as they reach the permissible age the final period in school should be outward-looking. Their studies must be interestingly and intelligibly related to the world of work, wages and young adult leisure they want to enter. This could of course be done in a comprehensive school, but if part of the purpose is to encourage them to feel that they are learning, but not now in a place for children, there is an argument for giving them a new kind of institution in which this could take place in an atmosphere that was new.

Now if we could make a perfect reconciliation between all these desirable things—and we obviously cannot—we should still have to relate what we could do to the facilities we have. There will be new building and some scope for deployment of staff. But what is on the ground now must affect what can be done, as has been pointed out. This, then, is our problem: to find the best common measure among different things that are desirable, and to get the best common measure between this and the facilities we now have or can provide.

It is important to get clear in our minds what we do want in any alternative system to selection at eleven. But of course it is easier to state general principles than to translate them into action. I think that not to cheat the reader I should give some indication of what might be done; repeating, however, that this will be a personal view, and that if readers would prefer rather different policies that will not affect my main argument as to the need for, and the nature of, right and relevant criteria.

Let us look at different kinds of school structure in terms of possible age-breaks. Some people would like the age of selection for an academic or non-academic secondary school to be made at thirteen. There are two arguments for this. Thirteen is at least two years later than eleven and we are that much better placed in relation to our first and second criteria. And secondly, thirteen is the age of transfer in the private sector from the preparatory to the Public school. If the two systems had the same age of transfer, movement from one to the other would be easier (the private system has little *differential* selection at thirteen, of course). These are good points, but there would seem to be some serious disadvantages also. The two years would be added to the primary school and it would be very difficult indeed in most areas to find this extra space in existing buildings. The result might be a diversion of a large proportion of resources away from the building of completely new schools to the addition of outhouses. Nor perhaps is thirteen a very good age for the top class of a school. Children are less homogeneous near this age than at most others in terms of maturity: some will still be children, others will be much more mature. Nor can one be quite happy about the next stage. The academic would go to a secondary grammar school for, normally, a five-year course; and the rest would go to a secondary modern school of only two years at present and of three years after the leaving age has been raised to sixteen. Two years is felt to be short for such a school and there must be doubts about a three-year school at this stage. In California where they changed from an eight-year primary school and a four-year high school to a six-year primary school they added a three-year junior high school and a three-year senior high school. The senior high school is considered to be a success; the junior high school much less so. And these junior high schools have not had "the cream skimmed off," as ours would.

Although thirteen has the deceptive air of the obvious next step there is probably more to be said for fourteen. This would permit the primary schools to remain undisturbed. From eleven to fourteen there would be a junior secondary school for everybody. At fourteen there would be a four-year upper secondary school for the academic and special two-year outward-looking education for those who were going to leave at sixteen. The proposals of the Newsom Report for such outward-looking education must be taken seriously. Merely to add another year of a kind of schooling they are already tired of will not do any good with these young adults. It will be difficult to give the kind of education that is wanted for them in existing schools, with their atmosphere and assumptions. And to some extent we shall have to recruit a special kind of teacher. All this, it is argued, could be much better done in a college devised for the purpose, a non-sixth-form college, so to speak.

These are fair, and indeed generous ideas. But there are serious objections to consider. The objection to the junior secondary school remains, and it is now stronger if the proposal is for a junior secondary school from eleven to fourteen. And are we so sure that at fourteen selection would be largely self-selection? Girls are said often to have made up their minds by fourteen. Yet there are many boys and girls at school now whose parents left school at that age. There is no very clear idea in many of these homes of the advantages of a continued school education, or of higher education after it. At thirteen or fourteen (indeed at fifteen, as the Crowther Report showed) young people who had the ability to continue did not think of doing so, with a serious loss of potential trained ability to the country. In a continuing secondary school they may discover themselves, realize that they could go beyond the technician to the technologist and that the professions need not be closed to them. If they have to make a decision between thirteen and fourteen they will be lost. And lastly, the inroads on the present structure would be very large indeed at the secondary stage. The secondary modern schools would disappear. Some would presumably become Newsom Colleges (fourteen to sixteen), most would become junior secondary schools (eleven to fourteen). That the secondary grammar schools would lose their pupils of eleven to fourteen is less serious; they could certainly survive as four-year schools.

All in all it seems as if the objections against fourteen outweigh the arguments for. More particularly, it is going to be extremely difficult to move towards this in two stages, first by making the age thirteen and then by making it fourteen. This can hardly be done, for the two years to thirteen would be added to the primary school; fourteen implies continuing with a primary school till eleven only and then making a three-year junior secondary school.

This seems to be leading us to the solution that at first must have seemed farthest away of all. What is really to be said against the idea of a common school to the age of fifteen or sixteen? If this were adopted the primary schools would be undisturbed; there would merely be physical transfer at eleven, not differential selection. Except in those areas where there was a full comprehensive system, the secondary modern schools would become comprehensive schools for every one up to fifteen or sixteen. This offers no serious physical difficulty. Three-quarters of the age-group go to them now, and in the next ten years the secondary school population up to the age of fifteen will be falling (the peak figures, for 1958, for the number of eleven-year-olds in the population, will not be nearly reached again until 1978). This, then, is the period when such a modification could most easily be made. And the "lift" that this change would give the secondary modern schools would be immense, contrasting markedly with their mortal bisection under the other schemes we have considered.

What would happen after this stage? I would favour the idea of the Sixth Form College for those who continued school education up to eighteen. They should leave to take this up at the age of fifteen as soon as our system of external examinations permits (a point I shall return to in a moment). Those who want to leave school at sixteen, however, would begin at fifteen a course of study—outward-looking and related to their adult work and interests—the first year of which should be at school and the last two of which should be part-time, while they were at work, the course being planned as a whole. The only serious inroads on present structure would be in the grammar schools, which under this scheme would lose their lower schools and become sixth form colleges. Again, the next ten years are the right period for making such a change, for the loss of the lower school would find compensation in the growing number who will be in school after the age of fifteen. I should like to say a word or two about each of these matters: the last year at the comprehensive school for those who will leave at sixteen, the sixth form college, and the effect on the grammar schools.

It is not easy to devise a course of study that makes a fusion between genuine education and the career and leisure interests of the young adult. Yet it is not in the least impossible. Psychologically what has to be done is to bring home the importance of study for almost any work or leisure that is worth while. Formally we must establish some sort of a continuum, or the school part of this will only be something to be got out of the way. The first year, i.e. the last year at school, should not be one of narrow vocational training, but to the extent of a half or more it should be pre-vocational education. The other half should be more general, but with freshly devised syllabuses for this special purpose. Into this the new Certificate of Education should fit. It is intended to be an examination on what has been taught much more than an examination to which the teaching has to be bent. (We have heard that before, but let us hope charitably that it is meant this time.)

But what, someone will say, about the "O" levels? More and more people are saying that they have had their day. At present, except for the "fliers" in some academically very good schools, they are taken at nearer sixteen than fifteen, after a five-year course. The sensible thing for those who are going to stay on till eighteen is not to have "O" levels that constitute a kind of first school-leaving examination—they are not leaving. What they should take is "O" levels later, covering the subsidiary subjects for which the "A" levels would be the main subjects. This was the pattern of the former Higher School Certificate, and it was what the Secondary School Examinations Council had in mind when it introduced "O" levels, though it made the mistake of withdrawing a proposal that "O" levels and "A" levels should be taken at the same time lest it penalize those who were re-sitting one or two subjects. Of course, under present pressures the great thing is to "get your 'O' levels out of the way" (i.e. end your general education as soon as you can). This is perverse, and with the hoped for lessening of the fierce competition to enter higher education the schools should be able to do rather better. "O" levels should not be a serious obstacle to passing at fifteen from a general secondary school into a sixth form college.

Why such sixth form colleges? First, because at this level the argument for separate teaching and learning gathers weight. Second, because the sixth form (as every sixth form master or mistress knows) is a distinctive stage in education. It is as different from the lower school as it is from the university, though perhaps it should be nearer to the latter in its intellectual temper and its methods of study. But we have too many small and ineffective sixth forms, far from the level of the very remarkable best. You must have specialized teaching in the sixth form and therefore, if you are to have a good range of subjects, a considerable staff. There are large gains to be had from a measure of concentration, especially in the country districts. Lastly, these more academic pupils are young men and women just as much as the Newsomites. One has a strong suspicion that many a young woman does not like wearing school uniform through to eighteen and that many a young man feels silly with that school cap on his head. There is little doubt that the sixth form college would be welcomed by most of the young people who would go to it.

There would of course be protest from the grammar schools, and it is right to see how far this would be reasonable and how far an outcry of mere conservatism with too little regard for education as a whole. Indeed the outcry that has attended the two or three such local proposals that have been made tempts one to suppose that the effort to teach the young to think objectively has exhausted the capacity of some of their teachers to do so any longer themselves.

The first argument is that if we are serious about the education of our abler children we must segregate them before the age of fifteen into separate schools. We have already seen that this is far from certain doctrine. Indeed some of the comprehensive schools that are still losing the "cream" at eleven because there are grammar schools or independent schools in their neighbourhood are already producing good enough sixth forms to make one doubt whether segregation is necessary between fifteen and eighteen, but if one allows that the case for segregation grows stronger as the age increases one can say with some confidence that up to fifteen there is little in this.

The argument that has emotional force is an institutional one, that the grammar school is an educational institution of proven worth and that to take away the lower school would be to destroy it. This is the argument that has to be disentangled. I think that what a good grammar school head feels is a certain pride in "standards," standards that he has a much better chance of inculcating if boys or girls come into the school young. If he analysed the word "standards" he would probably agree that he had in mind a blend of qualities, some intellectual, some moral and social, some matters of manners. Certainly there would be a respect for intellectual things, and a certain fostered firmness in adherence to them that it was more possible to cultivate in a segregated situation than in one where the vulgarities of commercialized appeals to the teenager might set the tone of a whole school. By moral qualities he would certainly mean that, by isolating his young from the world of delinquency and of the streets that presses more hardly on the modern school, although he would have his black sheep he could nevertheless give backbone to a good number of young people who without this reinforcement would not have become such reliable members of society. He would say the same about manners. Maybe the ethos of the grammar school is "middle-class," and in some of its manifestations it might be socially too conventional, but by and large its insistence on certain standards of manners are for the good of its own community and of society at large.

These are serious arguments. Unfortunately they get mixed up in practice with a lot of Speech Day stuff which, as critics have pointed out, is simply diluted Arnold. "I depend on my sixth form for running the school." Yes, but should they? And in what respects? There is in any case less in this argument at a day school than at a boarding school, because there is less to run. Dressing the prefects in a little brief authority has an artificial air in a day school; and it has been said that in a boarding school the kind of authority the prefects are given over the young is very much open to question. This is the wrong sort of leadership now. The kind of leadership one wants is that of the boys and girls who take on the running of the school societies and the school games and are more the choice of their fellows than of the head. Boys want leaders not officers; and girls no less.

It is also said that a headmaster depends on his sixth-form masters, his heads of departments, for ensuring a proper level in the teaching of their subject throughout the school. Here also one must try to distinguish fact from fiction. Some sixth-form masters and mistresses feel it to be good—or others feel it to be good for them—to teach for a part of their time in the lower school. While they are in a single large school this is good sense. But it is doubtful whether what they do really makes a major difference, an indispensable difference to preparing pupils for entry into the sixth form. A stronger argument is that their role as head of department keeps the standards up through their control of what their junior colleagues do. I think there is something in this. But at least two other countervailing points are commonly forgotten. The first is that this can have a wrongly conservative effect on younger teachers with rather newer ideas about how their subject can be taught. The conservatism of method of older grammar school teachers is notorious in some subjects (e.g. in modern languages). The younger teacher who comes out of training college or university department with serious ideas about modern teaching methods often has a frustrating time of it. A little more freedom for him or for her might be an advantage. And secondly the practice whereby the senior person is often (not always of course) the head of department and chiefly the sixth-form teacher is by no means necessarily right. Very often the intelligent young teacher, not perhaps yet experienced in the arts of class management, may be the right teacher for the sixth, and the more experienced man or woman, now perhaps a little farther from the frontiers of knowledge, may be better placed in the middle or lower school.

In weighing up what to do in face of these objections from the grammar school we have in the end to make an act of faith, based ultimately on our social values. The standards of the grammar school are on the whole good standards, and they have contributed to our society. But they are standards that have not permeated society. They have contributed in the first place, and directly, only to a section of society, one might now almost say to a class. To lose them and to gain nothing for society in return would be a serious loss. But the best secondary modern schools are making their contribution to right standards, too, and on a broader social front; and so of course are the comprehensive schools. To have the grammar school boys and girls, backed by their homes, in their schools would give them a great accession of strength. The question is, with all the forces that are arrayed against us, do we dare to say that we shall advance on one social front? Or do we say, that the battle is really lost and that the best we can hope for is a saving remnant to which we will give all the chance of social and intellectual leadership we can? I do not despise the arguments of those who take the latter view. But I do not despair of English society, and I take the former.

Let me, then, sum up the educational advantages of a structure of secondary education of the kind I have suggested, that is to say of a common school till fifteen, with a subsequent three years in a sixth form college for those who undertake to stay on and are recommended by their school to do so, and for those who wish to leave at sixteen one further year which would be followed by two years of related part-time education. First, we should have eliminated selection at too early an age and have turned it largely into self-selection. Second, we should have concentrated high level upper secondary education where the need for concentration is serious and the argument for segregation strongest. We should have fused the last year at school for those who left at sixteen with continued part-time education and young adult interests in work and leisure. And all this we could do (where there is not already a full comprehensive system) with little disturbance to our existing "plant" and less disturbance to our existing structure than any other plan, especially if we set about it in the next few years. These seem to me very considerable arguments.

Socially the gains would be no less significant. If the Swedes were asked why they have reformed their educational structure in the light of broadly similar ideas, they would unhesitatingly reply, "Because we want an educational system appropriate to our democracy." The only valid objection to this would be that a series of changes proposed militated seriously against educational development. In neither their case nor ours, it seems to me, does such an objection hold. With such changes as I have suggested we should have eliminated the false distinctions of prestige between general classes of school that have falsified the hopes of the Education Act of 1944, but we should preserve distinction where it matters. We should have done a great deal for promoting a sense of capacity to lead among those who were not necessarily academic, by leaving the top of the common school in their hands. And by bringing up all young people to the age of fifteen in a common school for work, play and friendships, we should have created a matrix for a much more democratic and less status-conscious English community.

If such changes as these were introduced into our public system of education we should still, however, not be able to say that education in England was democratic. The private sector of education, entrance to which (after passing the Common Entrance Examination) depends on ability to pay high fees, would make nonsense of such a statement. We have to recognize that in this private system, running from small preparatory schools to Eton, we have something the like of which cannot be found in any other country. There are some private schools in other countries, but nowhere do they so self-consciously serve a privileged section of society and nowhere do they afford such social standing to those who have been to them. It would be less than candid to pretend that they did not give these advantages to those who go to them, and these possible disadvantages to society as a whole.

This is so widely admitted that one rarely hears a straight defence of things as they are. A large number of those who teach in these schools have a social conscience about them, and from time to time some of them put forward proposals for modifying their social exclusiveness. But most of those who want some change, whether they speak from inside or outside the system, are reluctant to envisage any measure of compulsion. This may be illustrated by an extract from Mrs. Sybil Marshall's book about her experiences in a one-teacher village school in Cambridgeshire. She says—

> A social cross-section revealed that of these children, six came from "professional" homes; two had parents who were self-employed, one being the daughter of a hair-dresser and the other the son of a market-stall trader. The other eighteen were children

of farm workers or general labourers. The significant thing from this social viewpoint was the total absence of any representative of the farmer class. Such children went either to private schools in Cambridge or to expensive boarding schools where their ambitious parents paid high fees for the same education they could have got free on their own doorsteps. I would defend to the last ditch, the right of such parents to do what they considered best for their own children at their own expense, but it seemed to me that it did not augur well for the future health of the rural community that while the notable scientist's daughter and the eminent professor's son rubbed shoulders and held hands with their peers among the children of the labourers, the offspring of the accepted leaders of such a community were being educated, as creatures apart, in a town.[1]

Now the fact that a distinguished scientist and an eminent professor were ready to send their own children to Mrs. Marshall's school suggests that educationally they were satisfied with it. The fact that the farmers did not send their children, in spite of such unusual witness to the school's educational adequacy, suggests that their reasons were not educational but social. They did not want their children to mix with the children of the farm workers and labourers. It is very unlikely that their attitude would change because the village school teacher (even when as eloquent as Mrs. Marshall) said that it was a great pity. So in saying that she would defend their right to do as they were doing, and not use any compulsion, Mrs. Marshall was really acquiescing, though ruefully, in the continuance of this sad state of affairs. Is there any way out of this dilemma?

When we are in the presence of rival claims, both of which demand recognition as a right, but which cannot be fully recognized since they run counter to one another, we naturally look for some sort of a compromise. Hardly any one says that we should just abolish the private schools *en bloc*, much as

[1] *An Experiment in Education*, p. 29 (Cambridge, 1963).

Henry the Eighth dissolved the monasteries. The country is not in that sort of mood, and we are not that sort of society now. But, at the other extreme, do we think it good that not even for a small part of their school careers should the farmer's sons and daughters mix with the farm worker's sons and daughters? Do we think it essential, if we are to be one community to the degree we desire, that there should be such a period? I first heard the suggestion made by Mr. R. H. S. Crossman that if we leave parents free to pay for their sons to go to independent schools later they should at least have to send them to the general schools for a period of time. This would seem to be a very reasonable proposal. If, for instance, in Mrs. Marshall's village the farmer's children had had to go to the village school from the age of five to the age of nine those four years of rubbing shoulders and holding hands would have made a very real difference to the health of the rural community. Four years is not a negligible period of time. And such a proposal would not even mean the extinction of the preparatory schools, let alone the private secondary schools.

Now in a society like ours such decisions are usually made after a good deal of public discussion. If, for instance, there were a Committee on the Private Schools and they came forward with some such suggestion, opinion would gradually form, with a preponderance one way or another. It would be interesting to know what the farmers (and their analogues) would say. On what grounds would they refuse this measure of association with their fellow villagers? They could not seriously claim that their rights as parents were being abolished, for after the age of nine their children could go where they chose to send them, if they paid the fees. My own feeling is that the presence of their children at the village school would greatly help the school: if the farmer parents found there was no place for drying clothes in wet weather or no inside water something would be done about it! Equally the farmer parents would discover, as the professor and the scientist had, that the teaching was probably better than in the dame school that had been the alternative. Again, once this movement into the general schools had started, it is likely that it would go further quite voluntarily. Children who had been happy and done well at a primary school till nine might find they wished to stay, and the parents might say, after all why not?

In fact, we do not have to be quite so absolute one way or the other over obligations imposed by the state. I once heard a very good university lecturer asked whether he wanted a course of ten lectures he was to give to R.A.F. cadets to be voluntary or compulsory. He said that he wanted the first one, but the first one only, to be compulsory: he felt that in general they should be free to come or not to come, but they must first know what they were missing. The reply was unexpected, but much more sensible than a blanket answer in either of the two expected ways.

Much the same attitude is behind the suggestion about attendance for a period at the general schools. The lecturer I have referred to is said to have kept nearly all his audience for his subsequent voluntary lectures. I think it very likely that before too long the appeal of all but the best preparatory schools would diminish for a good number of parents. A few of them are very good schools; but by and large they do not have the same kind of educational claim that the better independent schools have. Parents know, however, that they provide the way into the private secondary schools, and especially to the big independent schools.

This leads us to the next step. One difficulty in making transfer possible from the publicly maintained schools to the private schools, or vice versa, has been that the two structures have been different in the age for movement from the primary to the secondary stage. An attendant difficulty has been in the subjects taught in the two primary stages: the publicly maintained primary schools have not taught Greek and Latin, whereas the preparatory schools have, and these subjects have been important in the entry requirements of the private secondary schools.

One attraction of the proposal to add two years to the public primary schools is that it would make the age for ending the primary period identical in the two systems as well as postponing the age of selection by two years. But, as we have seen, such a decision would create great problems in the public system. It would mean an age of selection that is still too early to be self-selection; it would imply the creation of a two-year "Newsom" school too early; it would not merely take off a top or a bottom from the secondary modern schools, it would cut them in two. Many people would feel that this was much too upsetting to the structure we now have. It would be better to encourage the better-staffed preparatory schools—or at least those of them that were open to a social appeal of this kind—to become schools from nine to fifteen rather than as now schools from about eight to thirteen. They would then reach the age at which boys and girls from the publicly maintained middle schools transferred to the grammar schools or sixth form colleges. It should be open to such schools to apply for "direct grant" on condition that they broadened their social catchment area and that mere private proprietorship gave way to a public trust type régime. And nine is quite early enough for starting Latin!

We now begin to see a structure emerging in the private sector which would enable the private schools to come much more into the general orbit of English society. What would be necessary to complete it is obvious: the Public schools would need to become sixth form colleges. This has already been suggested by Mr. John Vaizey. A new idea of this kind makes little impression at first. It is bound to look doctrinaire,

Utopian, unpractical, and all the other things new educational ideas are always at first said to be. But in fact this would not be so very big a step for the Public schools that above all pride themselves on their large and excellent sixth forms. It would also put proposals of the kind made by the Fleming Report in a new and much more acceptable light. There has never been much enthusiasm for the Fleming proposals to take a percentage of the population of the Public schools from the state schools. If, however, the changes suggested lower down the age range were adopted the intake of the Public schools at fifteen would have to be either from the publicly maintained middle schools or from the preparatory schools that went on to fifteen and had a semi-public status. The cost to the public authorities for three years post-middle school education would be less than the present cost of five years, and there would be a good case for offering three years of residential education at this age to boys who had till then been to a day school. After a while it is not at all impossible that a good number of the Public schools would see good in such a scheme. It seems at any rate much more promising than "Flemingism" as we have more or less considered it till now.

Some will say, however, that even though such a series of proposals would mitigate the present situation whereby the Public schools cater for, and tend to perpetuate a social *élite*, we should only be turning them into places for an intellectual *élite*. The two things seem to me very different. This is a matter which calls for careful thought—and not mere striking of attitudes—about our values. The kind of social *élite* which owes its position in the first place to wealth and has this confirmed by the inculcation of pride in a style of life distinctive of its own social club, is and must be distasteful to those who have a feeling for a genuine community. But hostility to an intellectual *élite* is Philistine. An intellectual *élite*, conscious that it is one, but feeling itself part of the community and not socially marked off from the generality of men, can be a great source of strength to a society. I don't think an intellectual *élite* that had been mostly at the general schools till the age of fifteen would offer any threat to a democratic society.

In this book I am concerned with principles, not with drafting detailed policies. I am only going far enough in that direction, with general indications of what might be possible, to illustrate the kind of solutions that are reasonable in a society like our own. The ideas behind these suggestions for bringing private more into relation with public education are based on a few assumptions that I should now like to resume. As with my suggestions for the public sector, some readers may agree with these assumptions and yet prefer different policy proposals from those that I have outlined.

First, it is legitimate to consider the effects on the society as a whole of a system of private schools within it. Secondly, it is legitimate to use a degree of pressure to secure a better total effect for society as a whole. Thirdly, we have to recognize that we are dealing with two or more rights that have to be reconciled; and therefore, in a society based on consent, neither abolitionism nor refusal to do anything is acceptable. More particularly, I have put forward for consideration the idea that it would be reasonable to expect every boy and girl to attend the general schools for at least a while (in my suggestion, the four years from five to nine), and I note that this could be done with no more disadvantage to the preparatory and Public schools than a delay of entry to the former by one year. Next I have suggested that if the people in the private system as well as those outside it would think of adapting the two structures to each other, in terms of age-breaks, this would help the two to come together; but personally I would sooner see the preparatory schools add to their upper range than the public primary schools go on till thirteen. I dislike the latter, not because it would not have advantages but because the other consequential changes in the public system would seem to be too great. Lastly, I have suggested that if the independent secondary schools became sixth form colleges they would retain what they rightly feel to be their greatest educational achievement and would be able to broaden their social intake without the disadvantages attendant on the proposals of the Fleming Report.

Needless to say, there would have to be much public discussion before such changes were decided on. Given our kind of society we should try to achieve as much as possible by agreement. But these private schools are a legitimate public concern. We really must admit that socially they are an anachronism, and not compatible with even the degree of general democracy we have, let alone the greater degree many of us might hope to have. But since also we respect individuals' rights we must try to propose a future that after discussion the socially-minded elements in the private sector will welcome without feeling that the educational good in them has been ignored.

VIII

EDUCATION AND ELITES

IT was the pride of ancient Athens, expressed by Pericles in his funeral oration for those who had died in the war against Sparta, that their society was a democracy, and a democracy that honoured excellence in men. The fear that democracy really means the domination of our social lives by a plebeian mob has induced in some sensitive people a distaste for the word and the idea, and has led them to defend a system of society in which the civilized values are in the custodianship of a ruling class or predominant caste. Others, who socially would be more sympathetic to democracy, have realized that what might be called democracy could be a system of society in which the masses with little critical resistance were exploited by an advertisement-based commercialism and they have seen our salvation in a cultured minority, not necessarily identical with a ruling class. The first of these kinds of social critic is distrustful of popular democracy in principle, and in consequence not enthusiastic at all about any large-scale extension of education. He doubts whether mass education could be what he understands by education. The second kind of social critic would welcome an educated and cultivated community as a whole but feels that the forces against it are too strong and has come to the conclusion that to attempt to secure it in conditions so unfavourable will only menace the survival of the cultured minority. So when it comes to the point of decision he also is against any large-scale extension especially of higher education. One might say that these two attitudes are broadly expressed by Mr. T. S. Eliot and Dr. F. R. Leavis.

It is rather a strange experience to read, or to reread, Mr. T. S. Eliot's *Notes towards the Definition of Culture*[1] in the present climate of ideas. It argues for a society much more highly stratified than any considerable body of opinion would now be willing to defend as tolerable, and it implies one much more static than would be possible even if it were. But it has qualities that make it still a good book to disagree with, not least that it is written in careful language. Mr. Eliot distinguishes between the culture of the individual, the culture of the group to which he belongs, and the culture of a whole society; but though he distinguishes between them he insists, rightly, upon their interdependence. Where the argument will seem to most readers to be unconvincing is in his middle term. Here his view of the family is important. He sees it as the most important agent for the transmission of culture, and in a much wider sense than might be intended by, say, a child psychologist. He has in mind a bond over a long period of time, and to gain the kind of transmission of culture he desires he has to postulate groups of families persisting, from generation to generation, each in the same way of life. Families of this kind group themselves into classes and must go on in the same place in which they began. Family, class, and local loyalty would in this way all support one another. This is a Burke-like view, to give its most recent possible analogue. The great oaks, the important families lending their protective shade to cultivated standards, are very much in mind. One would have thought this was to ask for a geographical and social immobility that would be quite impossible now.

This is not, Mr. Eliot insists, a defence of aristocracy. He dislikes the antithetical use of the terms aristocracy and democracy, and wants a society in which an aristocracy is one

[1] Faber, 1948.

part of society, with its peculiar and essential function. One can only say that such a society would not be a democracy, and it would be difficult not to regard it as antithetical to one.

The social backward look (for it is that, even though Mr. Eliot does not of course insist that the society he desires ever existed actually in the past) is associated with a cultural nostalgia. "We can assert with some confidence," he says, "that our own period is one of decline; that the standards of culture are lower than they were fifty years ago; and that the evidences of this decline are visible in every department of human activity." I should have thought this confidence to be very unhistorical. It could be defended within certain terms of reference (it could be argued, for instance, that the norms of taste were higher in the newspapers that were then bought than the average is now), but in other terms of reference it would be very much open to question (for instance, nothing like the volume of reading of non-fiction through our Public Library system would have been imaginable in the nineteenth century, and Mr. Eliot, understanding the association between high individual culture and the broader national levels, could not dismiss this as merely middlebrow and irrelevant as one suspects Dr. Leavis might). It is at least arguable, and many would so argue, that although the picture is a mixed one general cultural levels have not fallen, but improved since the period embracing the nineties and the rather vulgar Edwardian era.

Mr. Eliot also feels that high cultural standards, so far as experience till now can show, go with *in*equality of opportunity. And he brushes aside as a myth that a great deal of first-rate ability is being wasted for lack of education. The adjective "first-rate" of course demands some degree of definition, and greatly narrows what we might reasonably hope to assure. What simply cannot be asserted, in face of the kind of evidence that has already been referred to in this book, is that there is not a very considerable amount of potential ability that is being allowed to fail of fruition for lack of education. If we all had equal opportunities, Mr. Eliot feels, if we did without his middle term of groups and classes, we should have no nuclei of stability and coherence in society and would almost certainly be overwhelmed by a general vulgarity.

This at least has the merit of bringing to the fore the essential question. Do we think that *élites* (in the sense of groups of unusually gifted and able individuals) can command the respect and influence in a society that is necessary for the health of society itself if their special gifts and high standards are not mediated to general society through influential social classes? One could make a strong case for saying that the existence of such classes has prevented the working upon society of many gifted individuals; but leaving this point aside, can *élites* operate directly upon a society without being mediated through a privileged class?

Mr. Eliot agrees that since we have little experience of societies without classes this is in a degree an open question, but he makes it very clear that his fears greatly outweigh his hopes. I would agree that it is an open question and would go so far as to say that a "democrat" who considers his hopes a certainty is a very foolish person. In any society that moved decisively in this direction we might fail and there might be unredeemed low standards; and this could certainly happen here. But it depends on a number of things, the two most important being the capacity of a given *élite* to cohere enough in relation to its standards to make a general impact, and on the readiness of a society to concede respect and influence to admitted excellence.

We live in a very mixed society, but we have moved enough in this matter to be able to consider a certain amount of evidence from our own experience. Take, for instance, the level of musical cultivation. Whatever distaste we may have for "Music on the Light" and hysterical excitement over "pop" records, we are bound to agree that these things have not prevented a marked extension of enjoyment of serious and good music in recent decades. We do not have a real "Establishment" in music. That would be dangerous to vitality and development. And our musicians certainly do not come from, or become part of, a distinctive social class. But a series of organs in our society, from the Schools of Music to the Arts Council and the B.B.C. and the great festivals, assure our society good music continuously; and more people listen, and listen critically, to good music than ever. before in our history. Those who enjoy and value good music are not individuals lost in a vulgar mass. The composers and executants who form the *élite*, the discriminating listeners, and wider society, have a relationship mediated, not through a social class, but through functioning organs of our society of the kind I have described. An intrusion of a privileged social class whose decisions were decisive would be a gross impertinence. Would not any one be considered frivolous who said we could only hope to have good music if our composers and performers depended on great families making up a social class, and that supported musicians by inviting them to perform in their stately homes, having works dedicated to them in return?

The way of more widespread opportunity is surely the only way in which we can go forward. Most people would say that it is the way in which we should go forward. To attempt to return to a situation like that of the eighteenth century would be to deny music and hope of excellence in it to too many of our people. This is not Utopian and sentimental. It is those whose nostalgia suggests in spirit (though of course not literally) that they seek a Utopia in the past who may rather be charged with letting sentiment cloud their vision.

But this is indeed not to say that extension of mass opportunities will of itself give us a high civilization. That would be equally foolish. Many would argue (as I should) that without very strong social controls on those whose acquisitive drives lead them to exploit commercialized vulgarity our last state might be worse than our first. But apart from social controls of this kind, general education and its quality are all-important. In the general development of musical standards in recent years not only the Schools of Music but the schools in general have played a major part. In these many respects this experience of ours in regard to music does afford ground for legitimate generalization; and legitimate hope if we take the right social and educational directions.

The attitude taken by Dr. Leavis[1] will be felt, even by those who do not give his answer, to be nearer in some ways to the contemporary dilemma. Those who think with him have at least got two-thirds of the way to the stage of the French Revolution. That is to say that they would not wish entrenched privilege, based on wealth or birth, to dominate our society. They believe, in that sense, in liberty and equality; it is the fraternity that seems a trifle chill. But the French Revolution has, so to speak, operated through the Industrial Revolution, and they find that we now have a society that has lost the virtues of older communities, that has the apparatus of formal political democracy but is in fact governed more and more by the low standards of the mass advertising campaign. For this Mr. J. B. Priestley (and I know that both he and Dr. Leavis will feel it in doubtful taste that I should mention them in the same breath after all the critical sharpshooting of the past) has coined the term "admass." Now against this an education that gives serious critical standards is the best prophylactic. But—and here is the dilemma—this kind of education presupposes an intimate interpenetration of the minds of teacher and

[1] See the Sunday Times, August 19th, 1964.

aught, especially at the university level. Mass education is no remedy; only minority education can be, and if we rapidly enlarge our university population we shall only endanger the minority influences that are our best hope. Let us look at this view of Dr. Leavis.

The first thing to do is to get our history reasonably straight. It is a mistake to suppose that education, taken at its best, was better when it was restricted to fewer people than it is now. The eighteenth century is often described as the "age of taste" in English society, when the standards of wealthy patrons and the influence of a highly cultivated ruling class informed the life of the whole country. This is a very partial truth. What is certain is that in the eighteenth century the state of the private and Public schools was very low and that Oxford and Cambridge have never been so "unreformed" as they were then. In the nineteenth century—rather late in it as compared with Germany and France—we laid the foundations of a general system of public education. We now have a good standard in our primary education, and our grammar schools are incomparably better than they were in their pre-public days in the eighteenth and nineteenth centuries. The Public schools have as a group undoubtedly raised their academic standards in the last fifty years. As to the universities, Oxford and Cambridge were no doubt distinguished places and delightful to be in in the days before the First World War. But it would be difficult to argue that their standards of scholarship and research or of undergraduate intellectual achievement are lower now than they were then. In other words wherever you take our education now, looking for the best in each class—primary education, secondary education, university education—you will not find that the standards are lower than they were when education was confined to the few. On the contrary, there has been a general movement of society which has carried with it a great extension of education, and which has not diminished but has enhanced high achievement while extending its base. This is so obvious that one wonders how these critics who are so sure that more must mean worse have not noticed it and have not explained why a further extension now, especially in upper secondary and higher education, must have quite contrary effects from those we have experienced so far.

Reference is sometimes made to American experience to justify these fears. While we certainly have a good deal to learn from American experience, both by way of warning and by way of example, these kinds of comparison must not be made in an uncritical way. In the first place, we have to consider the general position in American society of the sceptical intellectual and not simply blame extended education for a scale of values imposed by society as a whole. But secondly we must be sure that we are comparing like with like. The assumed average in an upper secondary education available for every one will naturally not be the same as the standard attained in an upper secondary education reserved for a selected few. Nor can a college and university average be assumed to be comparable in situations where in the one case over thirty per cent of an age-group is involved and in the other some four per cent. Very often an English visitor to some not very notable campus feels that the atmosphere is not that of a university as he understands it; and he is quite right. But it does not follow that the better liberal arts colleges, the more distinguished private universities and the best state universities are doing work below that of the universities of Europe. That is simply not true.

There may, however, be conditions in which universal or near-universal education takes place that are not conducive to high intellectual standards. There may be high schools and colleges where the general sense of values is far from what it should be in academic institutions and where the gifted, and especially the critical and sensitive students in the humanities and the social sciences, are trying pathetically to flower in an alien soil. Many Americans have said that there is room for much disquiet about their high schools—though it is interesting to note that Dr. Conant says that the weaker high schools tend to be the smaller, not the larger ones, a point that "minority" educationists might ponder rather carefully. At the O.E.C.D. Conference at Kungälv in Sweden, to which reference has been made earlier, the American delegation was asked whether extension of education in quantity necessarily carried with it a threat to quality. The reply was commendably frank. It was that there was such a threat, but that it could be guarded against, and that the United States had not always done so and was increasingly conscious that it must.

Those who would restrict university education to about present numbers have a very difficult moral question to face. Unless they wish also to prevent more and more young people from taking their school education on into the sixth form, which one can hardly believe, they must be prepared to forbid university education to a large number of young men and women whose analogues a few years earlier would have had it and who are qualified, by the universities' own tests, to go on to it. This is an impossible position to hold. Our attitude should be a different one. We must begin by saying that this demand should be met: in the interests of society as well as of the individuals concerned. We should then consider the conditions in which the policy of expansion should be realized, recognizing that there is no inevitable threat to standards but that in the wrong conditions there could be such a threat.

Let me give a very obvious example. If expansion is unbalanced as between expansion of students and expansion of staff there could be such a threat. It has happened in India since independence. The easy thing is to say that the Indian universities have expanded too fast. The truth is that the expansion of student numbers has not been properly related to an expansion of staff and of general facilities for university teaching and study. The same looks like being true in France. This is not to say that expansion as such is wrong; but that to increase your students without correspondingly increasing your staff is as certain to lower standards as increasing the amount of money in circulation without correspondingly increasing the volume of goods is to produce inflation. There is nothing wrong with increasing the volume of either goods or money as such.

This distinction between an objective and the means taken to attain it is so obvious that one is puzzled at the failure to observe it. For instance, it has been argued that good university teaching depends very much on personal contact between tutor and student and on their both living and working in a congenial atmosphere; and that for this small tutorial groups and a reasonably small university are necessary. Let us agree. The implication that if we expand university education in the country as a whole every tutorial group must be too large to function and every university too large to give the right *milieu* is a patent *non sequitur*. The two questions are quite distinct. One is whether in total more students should go to universities. The other involves ways of doing this; and clearly you could (if you were so foolish) simply add the new students to your present groups and your present universities or, at the other extreme, you could leave these at exactly their present size and create for the new students new universities and new tutorial groups. The question of means has to be thought out on its own merits. As the Robbins Report makes clear, there are arguments for the large university as well as for the small, and the argument for either turns not entirely on generalities but on the possibilities of particular places in which the universities may be. Equally, in a large university you may or may not organize the teaching on the basis of small tutorial groups. The irrelevance of this question of method to the question of the total size of the student group is shown by the fact that the University of Sussex, which was the first of our new universities to announce that it proposed to race to the figure of three thousand students, has insisted on the tutorial principle in its plans for teaching. Why should any university teacher suppose that the statement "We ought to provide many more places for university students" means "I must greatly increase the number of personal pupils I teach?" It is very odd.

As we have seen, the ratio of staff to students in British universities is very favourable compared with other countries. It could fall a little without any serious danger, especially if more thought were given to methods of university teaching. It may be necessary for the ratio to fall a little to deal with the "bulge" in the next few years. But it must not fall much. And there is no reason why it should. We have got through the considerable university expansion of the post-war years without any general problem of shortage of staff, for the reason that we have here a self-regulating mechanism. If the number of university students increases, and the same proportion of them after graduating goes into university teaching, there will be the increased staff to teach the increased students. If that proportion falls it will be due to a diminishing attractiveness of the university career in comparison with other careers, and the remedy for that is the normal one—taking steps to make the careers of university teacher more attractive. There is no problem in principle that need defeat us.

The question of quality of staff is, however, more difficult. The number of first-rate scholars who are also first-rate teachers has always been small, and no doubt will always be. It is possible that their number will not rise proportionately as student numbers rise, at least if the assumption is sound that most of those who were potentially so doubly gifted have already been breaking through the barriers that have held back their slightly less gifted peers. There is no certainty that such fears will prove justified. There may be as good fish in the sea of ability as ever came out of it. But in any case a certain revision of our arrangements for the use of highly gifted teaching manpower is overdue. There is great virtue in the Oxford and Cambridge tutorial at its best, when both tutor and undergraduate are fully engaged; but one shudders to think of the total of hours virtually wasted in these one-to-one confrontations in the past when this has not truly been so. Nor should one forget that the distinction between teacher and research worker is of doubtful validity: some of the most distinguished and authentic teaching is done by the great research leader with his own research students. Yet again, it would be very wrong if a plea for a better use of teaching time led to a restriction whereby the acknowledged master of his subject taught only postgraduate students. These are all surely matters for intelligent discussion and arrangement. They, too, do not involve us in difficulties of principle.

One may say much the same about the right size of communities in which students live and learn and in which university teachers and scholars do their work. The Robbins Committee spoke of an average optimum size of a university as between eight and ten thousand. If that were accepted we should at once have to note that Oxford and Cambridge (where the fears seem strongest) have nearly reached that size already. To try to expand them to some twenty thousand would be misguided. Once again, this is a matter of sensible arrangements much more than of principle. The total size of a university is important, especially in relation to the place in which it is physically located. But this is commonly thought to be of greater importance than it is, and two other things are given less attention than they deserve. These are the belief that in university education personal contact is all important, and secondly that if you believe this you can do a great deal to plan for it, whatever the total size of the university. Oxford and Cambridge have a great tradition in this, not because of a more favourable ratio of staff to students, but because they have believed in it. Smaller institutions often have less of it, not (obviously) because they are too big, but because they do not believe so much in its value. It is just as obvious that if you want to provide smaller student and teacher communities within a large university it can be done. This is the great advantage of the college system, though that is not the only way in which it can be accomplished.

These things may indeed be pointed out by those who believe as firmly as any one that quality must not suffer in an expanded system of secondary and higher education. In the universities above all there must be this sense of fineness, spreading outwards into society but just distinct enough from general society to be immune from what might blunt its purpose. But we ought to ask what, in social terms, we want this quality for? Historically the ancient universities and the Public schools have been largely for the *formation* of the young of a governing class and of the more exalted professions. Do we now think that they should be for the *formation* of *élites*? If so do we mean by an *élite* more than a loose group of people, like our musicians, of distinction in a particular field?

We are of course a mixed society, with elements that derive from different stages of a long historical past and with others that are of our own time. One can still say that there is a class structure, though it is certainly not what Marx described in his lifetime nor what he predicted for the future. We could say that we are governed by a number of power-*élites*, and that these are not the same as social classes though they overlap with them.

A discussion of these terms, class and *élite*, and of the social theorists who have employed them, will be found in Dr. Bottomore's book, *Elites and Society*,[1] and he makes the point that in contemporary English society, however one defines these terms, the total number of persons who make the effective decisions is still surprisingly small, amounting at most to a few thousand. These are predominantly drawn from the upper and the professional classes, with due allowance for the possibility of entry into this number of persons who have come up from outside. In a footnote[2] Dr. Bottomore makes the link between this kind of society in which we live and its educational arrangements—

> In Britain, the typical careers of upper-class and working-class children may be described as follows: children of the upper-class are educated in the major public schools and at the Universities of Oxford and Cambridge, whence they proceed into business, politics, the administrative class of the civil service, or the older professions; working-class children are educated in state schools, for the most part secondary modern schools, from which they go at the age of fifteen, into manual jobs in industry or into minor clerical jobs, though some (a higher proportion today than twenty-five years ago) attend grammar schools and may go on to higher education in a provincial university or college of technology. Some children in each class may escape their fate, but the proportion who do so is too small to affect the general picture.

We have to ask whether on the whole these educational arrangements merely reflect the state of society, or whether they, so to speak, reinforce them backwards. If on the whole they reflect a less democratic complex than society as a whole, then it may well be that they are holding new forces in check more than they are liberating them for the health of society. But beyond this there is a further question. We ought not to be talking of power and influence only, but of the ends for which these may be used. Is our educational system rein-

[1] In this series, Watts and Co., 1964.   [2] p. 121.

forcing sound civilized values, and enough for us to have confidence that it could continue to do so even though it became less *élitist*?

The first question implies a decision in our minds as to where the balance should lie between what is common and what is differentiated. And one has to decide how far social divisions are, so to speak, artificially engendered by the educational system, and how far they must be so engendered if the educational system is doing its proper work.

If one says that there must always be *élites* in a society (thinking of an *élite* as a group with general social standing) one must mean more than the two statements (*a*) there must always be differentiations of work and function (*b*) some will always tend to direct and decide while others do not. Of course there must be differentiations of work and function in society, but the question is how far these carry differentiation of general social status. And in any given sphere there will always be a need for decision-making, however much collective consultation there may be; but the question again is how far the function of making decisions carries a generalized social standing with it. If a large farmer and an agricultural labourer live in the same village and both play cricket, and both moreover play for the village team, and the agricultural labourer is chosen as the captain and has no hesitation in not giving the farmer a turn with the ball though the latter fancies himself as a bowler, that is an example of division of function and decision-making without any suspicion of a social *élite*. It might just happen in an English village, but if it did you can be sure they would preen themselves on it over cocktails at the big farmer's and feel that the *noblesse* was indeed obliging. It would be an exception quite possibly to be approved, but to be remarked upon. The odds are that the farmer, if a tolerably good cricketer, would be the captain. And the odds are even bigger that he would not play for the village side but for his old boys' eleven or for some *ad hoc* club where there would be no social awkwardness in the dressing room. An *élite* in this sense is a social group that has not only an executive or managerial or ownership function, but a generalized social standing as a result of it.

It may be said that this is inevitable because there are working functions in society that rightly carry more prestige than others, and that this would be so even in a society that had caught up with the French Revolution and did not have feudal survivals. This is what Mrs. Floud has in mind when she says[1] that "Education is no longer as it was in Durkheim's day, a simple *corollary* of class or status position. It is increasingly a *determinant* of it." Mrs. Floud traces the difficulty we are in—apart from the feudal survivals—to the fragmentation of social experience brought about by occupational specialization. Your differentiated education, necessitated largely by the need for different kinds of training for people with different capacities, your specialization of employment, your professional group consciousness coming as a result, add up to a society that has fewer shared values than the idealist would desire. But can anything be done about this? Mrs. Floud replied that although participation in a common culture is bound to be selective and in this sense cannot be entirely common, nevertheless "we can surely envisage a communal culture—a culture in principle acceptable to all and communally sustained, as against a minority culture fed and perpetuated by an *élite*." And she sees the remedy largely in an education that is deliberately dedicated to the communal culture, whereas our own is deliberately dedicated to an *élitist* one. With this I would simply like to say that I wholeheartedly agree.[2]

[1] *Sociology and Education* (Sociology Review Monograph no. 4, Keele, 1961).

[2] *See also* RAYMOND WILLIAMS' admirable historical analysis, *Culture and Society 1780–1950* (Chatto and Windus, 1958).

Just as equality of opportunity must not be confused with equality, so a degree of mobility that permits a few to ascend to an *élite* must not be confused with community. Equally a desire for a genuine sense of community must not be confused with a desire to blur the distinction between what is excellent and what is not excellent at all. But how, in an educational system, can you discriminate between what is excellent and what is not and not begin to establish *élites*? If we mean by an *élite* not merely a group with a particular excellence, but a group that enjoys a generalized social prestige because of its function—then the short answer is, of course we can. In a sixth form the captain of cricket (to return to my homely analogies) of course enjoys prestige. So does the potential winner of a university open scholarship. But the latter may enjoy no prestige at all on the cricket field and the former may not be in the scholarship group. The recognition of specific excellence is to be commended; but what is also to be commended is the fact that the prestige accorded is in terms of the real excellence. It is not a generalized social phenomenon.

This, the pattern of a good school society rather than the Arnoldian sixth form oligarchy, is the right principle for a wider society. Our present educational system allows increasingly—though, as we have seen, much less than most people have supposed—for mobility so that a few more may join the *élites*. But it is at the same time becoming itself increasingly *élitist*. The big decision for us in education in England is along which of these two ways we intend to go. It is no more a decision as to whether we want or do not want quality in education than a decision not to have prefects as such but to let the captain of cricket and the scholarship candidate have their particular standing would be a sign of disapproval of excellence in cricket or scholarship in a school.

The differentiation of groups of different studies and kinds of study has led in English education, and most unfortunately, to generalized social differentiations far beyond anything that the economy or society can be shown to need. That there is some need for a balance to be struck is true. But a common school till eighteen with increasing differentiation towards the top, or (as I have indicated that I would prefer) a common school till fifteen with differentiation thereafter, together with the bringing into the general social orbit of the schools of social privilege, would turn us decisively from an *élitist* to a community direction There is no reason at all to suppose that with proper vigilance this should lead to a loss of educational quality.

But what does "a proper vigilance" mean? This question takes us beyond questions of mere organization and on to what is taught, and what values are inculcated, in the schools and the universities. On this I should like to say something in the next chapter.

IX

VALUES AND EDUCATION IN CONTEMPORARY SOCIETY

WE have seen that comparative studies constitute one of the necessary disciplines for thinking about education in relation to society. We are in fact continually making comparisons between our own society and others, and between their education and ours. However difficult it may be to make fair and just comparisons, the habit of trying to make them should be encouraged, for it is chiefly by comparisons that we discover what we think would be good in our own case. This value decision always remains for us to make: no mere information about education in the United States, continental Europe or the Soviet Union will do it for us. But information prompting comparisons does help us to focus more clearly on our own problems.

Comparisons may be across time as well as across space. No doubt serious historical comparisons are as difficult to make with validity as comparisons between contemporary societies, and to the careful historian any large generalizations are apt to be irritating for they leave out so many qualifications of which he is aware. Yet contemporary English society differs very significantly from English society in other periods, just as contemporary Western society as a whole differs significantly from societies of the past. To get our bearings, to see where we may be going now, we must attempt these large generalizations. If this is of interest to students of society it is no less of interest in education. Education can reinforce tendencies that social and economic change may be producing; equally it can counterbalance them to some extent if we decide that they are undesirable.

In a recent book[1] Professor Madge has made some broad generalizations about the characteristics of Western society as it has been developing in the last three or four centuries; and his generalizations are linked to his own value preferences. He asks whether the image of a society that we have in our minds is one with which we can be satisfied. To give a starting point in his discussion he recalls that Auguste Comte classified human societies into three historically successive kinds. He called the first stage theological, the second metaphysical, and the third and modern stage scientific, according to the kind of thinking that enjoyed most respect in each. Madge modifies these categories somewhat. He calls the modern stage not "scientific" but "rational-technical." This kind of society, growing in the West in recent centuries and now becoming worldwide, has certain obvious advantages over other societies; but Madge asks whether the dominance of the rational and the technical in our outlook has not had adverse effects on the quality of our living. He recalls the curious word used by Marx—"alienation"—to express his feeling that capitalist industry cuts men off from the sources of natural living and subdues their personalities to the unsatisfying work they have to do. If industrial work leaves us unsatisfied, may not the rational processes of thought behind it, the science on which its technologies are based and the often crude utilitarianism of its philosophy, deny something in our nature? Madge recalls that numerous otherwise divergent social thinkers have warned us against this. Not only Marx but Pareto, who insisted that we must not suppose ourselves to be just rational beings. Not only the sociologists but the psychologists, and in particular Freud, who revealed the part that the irrational

[1] CHARLES MADGE, *Elements of Social Eidos* (Faber, 1964).

plays in our lives and who warned us that, although we must control it, too rigid a control by the "super-ego" may bring its dangers. Madge himself would prefer a society in which the imagination had more scope and the aesthetic was more highly regarded in comparison with the technical.

Such questions, in one variant or another, have been asked about modern economic society from Burke to the present day and have often been accompanied by nostalgia for a past that may or may not have existed. With Madge's generalization there is no need to play the qualifying historian too much. We can agree about the importance given in the West to technical developments and we know that these have been based on the rational ordering of our experience through the sciences. This indeed is what we have chiefly in mind when we describe Western society as "advanced" and societies without these advantages as "underdeveloped."

These large-scale changes in the way in which we think and live have naturally been accompanied by changes in education. General statements may make the contrast too stark between, say, medieval and Renaissance thought, or even between life and thought in the Middle Ages and now. But there are major differences between medieval education and our own. No one now would think of theology as "the queen of the sciences." The whole patterning of thought has been radically changed since the age of scholasticism, and the methods of thinking appropriate to our times have gradually made their way into education and have become generalized and made fruitful for further developments through education. Qualifications to the effect that the thinking of scientists is not only inductive, or that the modern age was not only different from the medieval period but of course also grew out of it, do not invalidate the main generalization. The experience of being educated at school or university now is so different from what it was that we may fairly say the student then inhabited a different kind of intellectual world. This is a broad change that is familiar enough.

But every half century or so shows some further modification of our education within the general pattern, and there is a close (but not absolute) correlation with the general development of our technological society. Thus the last hundred years have seen the displacement of the classics from their position of extreme domination and the establishment of the pure, though not yet the applied, sciences in a position of great prestige in our schools and universities. We have seen the gradual establishment as subjects of repute of what might be called the new humanities. Arnold introduced modern history into Rugby, and following history English and other modern languages and literatures have won their place in the universities as giving a basis for a liberal education which it was once supposed the classics alone could give. We are now witnessing an increased demand for the social sciences in higher education. Perhaps the most interesting feature of our time is, however, the struggle of the applied sciences to establish themselves as reputable: they have virtually achieved this now in the universities (where in any case they have long been present, if not universally accepted) though it remains to establish their standing in the sixth forms of academic schools.

In all this it would seem as if education were just following behind social developments, and at a pace that was perhaps regrettably slow. But it is not so simple. Education has its own voice in the conversation. The economy may "demand" that this or that subject be studied, that training be given for this or the other vocation; but those whose reponsibility is the education of the young will reply that this may be all very well but they have something else to consider. They are concerned not only with supplying the economy with producers, or even with furnishing citizens to the state, but with educating men and women. So there is a perpetual dialogue, in which (after overcoming a certain conservatism) the schools and the universities reflect a growing social or economic need but in which they also add something of their own which permits the assimilation of these innovations to larger and more permanent aims. Let me give an example of the kind of interplay between technical developments, social values, and education that I have in mind.

Because we can exert more control over our environment now we feel less helpless in the face of threats to our security and therefore put more positive value on intelligent action and less on passive acceptance of our fate than previous ages did. The fatalism that we associate with traditional Islam, but that is also a feature of traditional Christianity, is maddening to a reformer who can see that some science-based action could deal with a danger before whose supposed inevitability there is no need to bow the head. If there is a water-borne disease, we look to the water supply and don't just say: "it is the will of Allah" or "the Lord giveth and the Lord taketh away." Hence resignation in the face of circumstances, once regarded as a high spiritual value, is less regarded than reasoned forethought and action that would once have attracted a charge of impiety. Indeed, now, one of the more puzzling things in the Jewish-Christian myth of the Fall to a child in school, where he knows he has been sent to get knowledge, is that it was the Tree of Knowledge of which Adam and Eve were told *not* to eat. To get knowledge, his school ethic tells him, is to rise, not to fall. Man, "still aspiring after knowledge infinite," is a modern not a medieval ideal. Hardly any one now would deny that it is a positive duty of education to encourage such an outlook and to foster habits of mind that discourage resignation before difficulties in our environment. Every one from a Western country who has taught in a school in an "underdeveloped" country knows what this means. We must use our reason more, and develop our techniques further, and the idea that there is a risk of "sin" in this, or an overweening pride that will bring Nemesis in its train, is felt to be nearer to superstition than sense. Medical missionaries from modern to backward countries usually end up more medical than missionary.

But this does not mean that the Book of Job or the great works of poetic tragedy are out of date. We may guard better against immediate dangers. But the ultimate human situation in the universe has not changed, and there is no reason to suppose it will. There is a mystery to which we must make an imaginative and a moral adjustment. Medicine has developed, but we still have to die. Now the fact that we use our reason increasingly to guard against immediate dangers does not mean that we cease to feel these ultimate things, any more than it means we cease to respond to the delights of life. This is sometimes supposed to be so because such responses have often been in terms of beliefs that are held now with waning force. But when the abandonment of a belief has gone the whole way, we see that it is only the form not the response that has disappeared. There is no reason to suppose that an astronomer responds less to the beauty of the stars than some one who still believes in astrology, or that one cannot respond to the *Iliad* or the *Odyssey* unless one believes in Apollo or Pallas Athene. The use of the rational powers of the mind to change an unreasonable attitude or belief carries no necessary threat to the imaginative or the moral life. Yet such fears still impede the application of reason to human affairs when it is very much needed.

This should be understood in education. There is, however, a danger against which it is necessary to guard. Through the pressures of a society, or of a religion or of a philosophy, it is possible to produce a terribly one-sided education, and therefore an unbalanced man or woman. The hostility of certain religions to the teaching of evolutionary biology is a classic case of the inhibition of the rational—whether with any compensating imaginative or moral gain may be doubted. The account given by John Stuart Mill of his own education on the utilitarian principles of his father, so that his mental health was saved only through the imaginative release of the poetry of Wordsworth, is a classic case of the over-emphasis of the rational. This means that in any social situation those in charge of education must not follow economic or social or philosophical tendencies blindly. They have an independent duty to ask of themselves whether the education they are giving is right in terms of the whole man, or if you like in terms of values that are more permanently human than the particular pressures of the moment allow. According to circumstances, the good teacher may be fighting for the right to inculcate rational processes of thought against established stupidity—Scopes versus William Jennings Bryan; or he may be fighting for imaginative expression against crudely "practical" controllers—on the side of Sissy Jupe against the Gradgrinds of the day; or he may be standing for something moral—the Good Life versus good sales.

Because of these things the teacher has a peculiarly difficult task. He is part of contemporary society and has a duty to it. But he is not to be subdued by it. He has to ask what the values of his society are and which of these he would wish education to reinforce, which to modify or even to combat.

Our own contemporary society is no more to be dismissed with lamentations than it is to be accepted with uncritical praise. There have been many worse societies; less comfortably provided, with a poorer cultural heritage, more ignorant, less tolerant. If we begin our reflection on the values we would like our society to express by noting those it expresses now, we do not start too badly. In many ways change has meant undoubted improvement on the past. In other ways we may well have lost something good; and the forces of change that confront us now bring very real dangers, from the spoiling of our once lovely countryside and townscape to the vulgarization of standards by subtly dishonest advertising. We do have very difficult questions to consider. What are the values in our society for which we should expect education especially to stand?

They would seem to me to be of four main kinds. First, from its very nature, education must stand for intellectual values. Professor Madge, seeking for adjectives to characterize our modern society, finds one in the word "rational." The word "intellectual" is rather wider than this, and I prefer it as distinguishing the contribution of education to society that is perhaps most special. Secondly, we expect education to foster what are sometimes called the values of a liberal mind. These include intellectual values, though it is possible to think of an "intellectual" who is not really liberal-minded. In particular, we have to consider how education is to meet the need for liberal values in an age that Madge also characterizes as "technical." Then thirdly, education is always expected to contribute to the moral development of the young, and the moral values that should inform it are very much under discussion at the present time. Lastly, there are what might perhaps be called the values of community, for education is also expected to help each generation to feel itself part of society. This again is not to be altogether distinguished from moral education, for it is part of it; but it is worth separate discussion.

Questions about the role of education in inculcating these values are obviously large ones, no doubt much too large to answer properly in the concluding pages of a book like this. But they are the most important questions of all to ask about education and our present society. I should like at least to raise them, and to give some indication of what my own answers would be, before bringing this book to a close.

1. The Intellectual Values

Educational institutions are a most important agency for "socializing" the young, and writers like Durkheim who have emphasized this have included in their notion of "socializing" the inculcation of habits of thinking desired by a society. But "socializing" is often thought of as much more a matter of inducing emotional adjustment and of internalizing norms of social behaviour in the child. It would be foolish to under-estimate the importance of this. It would be equally foolish to forget that children and young people cannot learn properly if they are emotionally disturbed or deeply unhappy. Educational institutions have their part to play in both these matters. But this is not distinctive of them. There are other social groupings and agents that are concerned with these things. In enthusiasm for these roles of education it is sometimes forgotten that schools, colleges, and universities have one role that is quite distinctive: it is to teach the young to *think*.[1] There is no other social agency that has the responsibility for doing this systematically.

People without any formal education may, as we know, be quite well-adjusted emotionally to their society and they may be stable and happy persons. Their reflection on their experience of life may bring them a kind of wisdom. But unless they have had some formal education it is most un-likely, except in the most primitive biological way, that they will have learned how to think. For this, formal and systematic training is indispensable.

[1] Mr. T. S. Eliot makes this point (op. cit., p. 99): "What we remark especially about the educational thought of the last few years, is the enthusiasm with which education has been taken up as an instrument for the realization of social ideals. It would be a pity if we overlooked the possibilities of education as a means of acquiring *wisdom*: if we belittled the acquisition of *knowledge* for the satisfaction of curiosity, without any further motive than the desire to know; and if we lost our respect for *learning*." I entirely agree and would only add that although his use of "social ideals" as separate from educational pur-poses in intelligible, I would feel any social ideals poor if they did not include these.

The prerequisites for future intellectual power need to be encouraged early, and they are for the most part best encouraged by not insisting prematurely on formal academic learning. Hence the paradox, so familiar to teachers and still baffling after the baby stage to many serious-minded parents, that the right kind of work for young children is play. (Indeed a kind of capacity for play, for playing with ideas as we say, is to the end of his days a faculty of the man who is at ease in the world of ideas.) But as a child matures, and he becomes able to grasp such notions as cause and effect and to follow logical processes, his intellectual development becomes more specifically the concern of the school. In the secondary school and the university this is so much so that we know that if it is not looked after properly, whatever else may be pleasant or good about these places, they are failing in their distinctive work. For secondary schools and universities a failure to honour the intellectual virtues is the decisive betrayal, the sin against the Holy Ghost.

"Ah," some one will say, "but you are talking of the *élite*. This will do for the secondary grammar schools and the universities, but when everybody stays on at school you cannot realistically set such an aim. You must interest the others, of course, give them some useful knowledge and some skills, and help them generally to mature. But that is all you can do." I would contest this and on three grounds. First, I believe that all young people who are not positively subnormal should find in the ordinary schools the fullest opportunity to develop their intellectual potential, whatever it may be, because it is their right. Secondly, they need this for coping with life. And thirdly, if we do not make great efforts to give them this they will take their revenge on the *élites* and society will become unfit for the *élites* to live in.

None the less this objection poses for us one of our capital present-day educational problems. Let us assume for the moment (I shall come back to the point) that we do inculcate the intellectual values reasonably well in our sixth formers and our college and university students. What can we hope to do (and how can we do it?) for the "Newsom" boys and girls?

In the first place let us be clear as to what we are not doing. We are not arguing that all children and young people should follow the same "academic" curriculum. There may be subjects of study that are too difficult for some children: some branches of mathematics for some, Greek and Latin for others. Still less are we suggesting that all boys and girls should be taught by the same methods that are used for the clearly academic. What we are talking about is the aims of teaching, however appropriate different methods may be with different children.

We can go further. It is true that not all children are equally promising in the capacity for abstract thinking, for the grasping of theoretical concepts. But because a person is not an intellectual or a theoretician it does not follow that he is a fool. And if he is not a fool he has learned not to be one. How has he done this? He has acquired relevant knowledge and has been trained, by teaching or direct experience, to adopt a critical attitude. He has developed a certain capacity for judgement—something that some theoreticians and intellectuals may well not have. Now with young people who are not at home in the world of theories and abstraction this is what we must rely on if we are to encourage them to think. And the process will only succeed if the acquiring of such knowledge and the development of critical attitudes interests them. "Relevant" knowledge means relevant to their needs and to their interests. These may not be the same, but they are commonly nearer than our teaching allows.

The Newsom Report, in saying that the last year or so at school, for those who do not intend to continue their full-time education after they have reached the leaving age, should be outward-looking, recognized that interest would not be in learning for its own sake or for an ultimate professional goal. It would be of two more immediate kinds. In the first place, those young people who want to get out into the world know they will have to earn a living in it (or be the wives of those who do) and this fairly soon; so, though they do not all know what kind of work they want to take up, their interests are largely vocational. When we say that there can be vocational education in school but that school is not the place for vocational training, we mean that schools should not merely train in skills but through the skills should teach something of underlying principles and invoke broader interests. The latter especially relates to the concept of a liberal education in relation to technical training, and we shall come to that in a moment. But our immediate concern is whether we can teach young people to think, to reason, through the learning of skills. (We can dismiss the question: should we, if their work is going to be repetitive when they do get a job? Apart from the fact that the man who thinks about what he is doing is bound to be a better operative, that it is the totally unskilled man who is in danger of technological unemployment, and that automation will make the need for unskilled workers smaller and smaller, we must say that in the interest of the man as distinct from the producer we must get his mind working.) It is true that some subjects are easier to teach educationally than others, the mechanics of a car, for instance, than typewriting or shorthand. But the educational device to be used in the latter case is to place the learning of the skill in a wider context, and maybe to make no educational bones about the skill itself but to go for it in a rapid intensive course first just because it is necessary. But in truth there are very few subjects likely to be asked for in schools that do not lend themselves to stimulation of thinking, if the teacher knows that that is what he is to do. There is always the type question: "Is it better to do it this way or that, and why?" on which a hundred variants can be played. But of course the dull teacher thinks this interrupts the learning of the skill and finds it simpler to say "Do it this way."

Undoubtedly a wider range of possibilities is opened by the second kind of immediate interest of young people soon to leave school. This is in the world into which they are going. Here we are failing almost entirely to develop any kind of critical thinking that will stand these young people in good stead. There are experiments in some schools, often showing enterprise and imagination. But by and large we have not thought this problem out, and we have not deliberately trained teachers to do it. If the higher school-leaving age comes into effect before we have done so the result will be not merely wasteful, but disastrous.

Now there are teachers of the social sciences in the universities who say that they do not want these taught in schools; and there is a sense in which they are right, from their own point of view as university teachers of these complex subjects and from the point of view of the young in school. Below the sixth form at the very least, one does not want economics, sociology, psychology taught, as subjects with their own theoretical structures and disciplines. But one does very badly want descriptive teaching about the world into which these boys and girls are going. They should know more than we tell them about the world of work and wages; they should know a little about everyday finance (what a cheque is, for instance, or what a balance sheet is, or the difference between capital and recurrent expenditure); they should think about the supermarket in relation to the little shop around the corner; they should know about some of the significant social changes of our time; they should know what trade unions, and consumers' associations, and political parties are. And this should be taught, not in terms of abstractions, but in terms of personal experiences and actual events and problems. Why are the workers in a given industry on strike? Should women have equal pay with men? What does the headline "Trade gap widens" mean? Why have prices gone up as compared with a year ago? What is the United Nations, and why is there a United Nations Force in this or that trouble spot? Do international sporting events make for better understanding between the different countries or don't they? "Civics" is no new subject. Nor is any one of the examples I have given undiscussed in some school somewhere. But we have not developed systematic methods and assembled comprehensive materials for this kind of teaching.

As we saw when discussing different possible school structures, there is a strong case either for a separate "Newsom College" or for a final year at school clearly differentiated from the rest, not only for the boys' and girls' sake but to get fresh initiatives into the teaching. "How can I do this when there isn't a proper textbook?" Maybe it would be better not to have a textbook, but to base teaching on critical and comparative reading of three or four newspapers, with an appropriately stocked school library to back these up and take study beyond them.

It is not true (let me repeat) that only an intellectual can learn to be critical. A few schools have made a point of studying advertisements critically, usually in the English lesson. There could be few more effective inducements to critical thinking—and the teacher's material is of course unlimited here. There is no need to labour the point. If we know our aim to be, not to fob off the supposed dullards with woodwork or typewriting (which is more than a little of an insult anyway) but to give every boy and girl to the limit of his capacity the critical awareness he needs, we shall do both him and our society great service, and the pedagogical problem can be solved by hose with initiative. It is the aim, the attitude, that matters.

But are we quite sure that all is well higher up in the intelligence range? After all, this is where the important decisions for our future as a nation will have to come from and there is not too much room for complacency. There is no doubt, of course, that in our sixth forms and our universities the intellectual values are honoured, and highly. We may not put quite the same weight on sheer learning as the Germany of tradition, or develop such individualist reasoning power as the French, or have the same zest for new procedures as the Americans, but on balance we need not feel ourselves inferior to any. Yet what does our society now need?

It would not be too much to say that we are at one of those periods in our history when, industrially, socially, and intellectually, either there is a renewal, or we belong to the past. We enjoyed such a renewal, in common with the rest of western Europe, at the end of the Middle Ages. We found the capacity for it, rather more in our own right, in the second half of the seventeenth century, when we achieved a compromise in society and government that healed the wounds of the Civil War and took us forward to a great age with a new positive impulse, symbolized intellectually by Newton, and the Royal Society, and tempered by the tolerant philosophy of Locke. We found such a capacity again in the middle years of the nineteenth century, when we left behind the fading elegancies of the Regency and, if we had a stuffy and rather conventional Victorianism, had nevertheless a new industrial and civic energy, a new sense of moral purpose, and an immense reform of our educational institutions. In all these cases an intellectual and a social movement fused together to take us into a new age. One begins to wonder now.

We have prided ourselves that although we are less given to the merely rational than the French, we foster judgement and "team spirit" more. There is truth in this. This is appropriate for "broadening down from precedent to precedent"—and we have undoubtedly been good at that. But there comes a time for more daring ideas. One difficulty from which we suffer is that our life, where it is most intellectual (let us say in the sixth forms of our very best schools and in the Universities of Oxford and Cambridge), is most subdued by the complacencies of the *status quo*. The Public schools will tolerate an occasional radical, Oxford and Cambridge rather more, but the life-giving ideas run into the social sands. How is it that although our secondary schools and universities at the undergraduate level are incontestably more intellectual than the average American high school or college, yet on the whole (and, one must add, outside the conformism of social behaviour) America often provides an atmosphere of forward-looking excitement in the world of ideas? May this, in the end, be one of the advantages of that common effort in education which, in the shorter run, has disadvantages which we all too easily see?

One disappointment, it must be admitted, has been with the general educational effect of the rise of science. It is unfashionable to say such things now. But the truth is that the increased standing of the sciences has not had the general educational effect we were assured it would. What was the argument? That scientific thinking was appropriate to the new age; that the study of science would spread the benefits of the scientific approach in a general way. We should learn to look at the evidence first, to experiment where experiment was possible, to test every tentative hypothesis we formed, to be more rational about human life. It has not happened. If you asked for critical and objective discussion of a social or human problem, with respect for the evidence and rational processes of thought, you would be more likely to find it among the history and the arts sixth, or their later equivalents in the universities, than among the students of the physical sciences.

This may be because science is so much taught, in no sort of accordance with the myth, but as received knowledge, so that principles disappear under a weight of data and facts. It may be that science has to abstract and that the laboratory situation cannot be reproduced in the world outside. But I think it is broadly true that the "transfer" rarely takes place. On the whole, to put it at the most modest level, scientists show no more critical capacity than the rest of us when they deal with life and affairs outside their laboratories.

Yet I still think the hope is valid. In the much longer perspective there has been this carry over from science. The belief in witchcraft began to die in the period in which the Royal Society was founded. There are always scientists who try—the "Pugwash" movement is the most recent example—to think scientifically over the wider human range. But in the schools and the universities we have failed for two main reasons. One is the pressure that, as I have already noted, has led to sacrifice of scientific principles for accumulated fact. That, given the will, can be remedied; and there is now a significant reform movement in science teaching. Secondly, our education has been grotesquely over-specialized. How can we expect the sixteen- to twenty-one-year-old scientist to make a transfer of his habits of mind beyond the laboratory if we never give him the conditions in which this can be done? If the laboratory situation is rightly abstracted from real life, and if in real life we have to learn how to make decisions where evidence can never be conclusive, the sovereign study is that of history and social and political affairs. We cut scientists off from this at the age of fifteen or sixteen.

To sum up. The intellectual values are not unhonoured in contemporary English society. If "intellectual" is a term of doubtful praise with us, at least "egg-head" is not a term of abuse. But the effects are not as pervasive as they might reasonably be. We have not faced the problem of giving the academically less gifted the critical awareness of society without which society must be the poorer. In the sixth forms and in the universities (and since they are socially honoured, also in society at large) we respect the intellectual virtues; but through both our educational and our social complacencies we muffle the effect, so that we are in danger of not getting the vigorous renewal of our national life that, now the world terms have changed so decisively, we badly need.

2. *Technical Education and Liberal Values*

This problem, like the one we have just been discussing, involves a value choice in a social setting. We have no doubt to decide how far the popular antithesis between a technical education and a liberal education is a valid one. But having decided to what degree it is valid, and there is in consequence some pull of rival interests, we have to understand the social and economic factors that make technical education so important for us. Having studied these factors as far as we can, and having studied them in the realization that our present position is different from what it was in this country in the past and different at least in some respects from what it is in other contemporary societies, we have to discover a rational basis for the value balance we decide to strike.

What are the relevant economic and social factors? The first, obviously, is that our society depends on technological development. This in turn means that from year to year a higher proportion of our labour force needs technical training and the general education that is a necessary prerequisite of it. Next, because we are having more young people at school longer than we formerly did and also increasing the population in higher education, we must expect a higher proportion of those taking upper secondary and higher education to be vocationally minded, a great number of them with technical or technological careers in mind. In these circumstances what happens to the concept of a liberal education? We must examine the term itself a little more closely.

Happily, when the term is used now it does not set up in the hearer's mind an antithesis between the sciences and the humanities. Few people now would dispute the proposition that a study of science as well as of the humanities is necessary to liberate the mind from the tyranny of ignorance and of the immediate and must therefore be part of a liberal education. But this is not so easily asserted of the applied sciences, and least of all will it be easily accepted of merely technical education, which a hostile critic might say was the applications without the science.

Now "liberal education" is a term with heavy social overtones. Indeed there could not be a clearer example of the vanity of trying to think of education apart from its social setting. As we know, the concept was first discussed seriously in ancient Athens, and our ideas about it have been influenced especially by the views of Aristotle. He was concerned with the kind of education suitable for a free citizen. Since in Athens most of the hard work was done by slaves and household affairs were looked after by the women, citizens were free to think of the part they should play in government and above all of the use of their leisure. Aristotle ruled out education for servile tasks and he frowned on education that prepared one for a commercial career. A liberal education, therefore, was one that prepared a man for a cultivated and public-spirited life. This at least is the popular account with which we are familiar. It does, however, need a few qualifications.

One can generalize overmuch about Athenian society from Aristotle, and one can take Aristotle himself a little out of context. He was not designing an education for the idle gentleman: he would have had contempt for the eighteenth century aristocrat who said "As for living, our valets will do that for us." He was educating for an active and socially responsible life. As to the Athenian attitude to work, we should remember that Plato, who was very much an aristocrat, took for his master Socrates, who was a stonemason; and this does not seem to have set up any distaste in Plato's mind at any time. Plato himself believed that each kind of specific responsibility should be given to those who have aptitude for it and have been trained to discharge it. He, too, thought that the distinctive social activity of the free man would be government (though his highest mental activity was philosophy). But though we want a captain of a ship to know his navigation and a doctor to know his medicine, the common run of politician in a democracy does not understand what the purposes of government are. To this degree Plato believed in professional training. It is not really true that even Aristotle was opposed to all useful studies. He said: "That such useful studies as are absolutely indispensable ought to be taught is plain enough ... We can describe as mechanical not only those arts which degrade the condition of the body but also all mercenary employments, as depriving the intellect of all leisure or dignity."[1] If Aristotle were with us now, returning in ghostly fashion for an evening's talk, we might reasonably put it to him that thanks to our technological progress very few jobs need now degrade the body and that many occupations that seemed not indispensable to him, such as commercial ones, were indeed indispensable to us, and that his conclusions might change therefore in terms of our society.

The distinction of his time between the slave who had to work so hard that he was no more free in mind than in body, and the free man who did not need to work, has disappeared. Now we are all free, and we all have to work. (The paradox is that soon we may be back in Aristotle's position at least in the sense that what to do with our leisure will be a most difficult

[1] *Politics*, book V, Ch. III (Welldon's translation).

problem.[1]) But it is only in recent times that we have reached the point where the old Aristotelian distinction has ceased to hold. Indeed, up to the outbreak of the First World War the idea of the cultivated man of leisure had just enough basis in English social reality for the Aristotelian conception to have great appeal.

This Indian Summer of English traditional society fostered a parallel Indian Summer of Aristotelian ideas of education. Of course English society was very different from that of Aristotle's Athens. What made possible an approximation to Aristotle's ideas in this setting was a concept of which Aristotle would have made little, that of the "liberal" professions. Aristotle distinguished between the life of the free citizen and professionalism of any kind. But nineteenth-century English education, upholding the ideal of the amateur rather than the professional in most things (and especially in games), nevertheless recognized certain professions as within the range of the gentleman. The merely mechanical was not respectable, the industrial was very doubtful (though its fruits might be enjoyed, especially in the second generation), the commercial was viewed with distaste: the technical was out. But the "liberal" professions were the essence of respectable society. Only possession of land in large quantities gave greater standing.

Thus there was undoubtedly a social distinction between the liberal professions and other callings. But a second distinction was educational and is of more permanent interest. What entitles us to call one profession liberal and another not? Abraham Flexner in his book on universities[2] said that what made a profession was that it was learned; it involved a *corpus* of knowledge that was of interest for its own sake and an intellectual attack on problems. This is true of the liberal

---

[1] *See* Professor Dennis Gabor, *Inventing the Future* (Secker and Warburg, 1963).

[2] *Universities: American, English, German* (Oxford, 1930).

professions we have mentioned, which were essentially the learned professions; qualification for them involved academic study and not merely vocational training. In the schools and the universities this was the real defence of the distinction between study leading to them and to other callings.

This distinction has failed to hold. The position of medicine was always equivocal in any case, for a degree in medicine did involve vocational training as well as theoretical study, though you could take premedical studies as it were for their own sake during the university part of the training. Inevitably the applied sciences made their way in, though the distinction was maintained between the degree and the professional qualification, as in law. But increasingly degrees have been given, in whole or in part, for studies with a clear vocational implication: in dentistry, commerce, agriculture, and now indeed in a far greater range of studies than the traditionalist is aware of. We have not quite reached the stage expressed by the words of the Founder at Cornell: "I hold a university to be a place where anybody can study anything." But we are nearer to it than we were. (Cornell University is at Ithaca in the State of New York, named after the island home of Ulysses. Homer, Ulysses, Athens, Aristotle, Ithaca (N.Y.)—the wheel has indeed come an ironical full circle!)

We in fact agree now that our traditional position has become a little absurd. We have agreed that the Colleges of Advanced Technology shall have university status, and that those who emerge from them shall have, not diplomas, but degrees in technology. This gives a recognition that is overdue; but it does not solve our educational problem.

Most of the heads of these institutions, and many heads of technical colleges, are anxious to broaden the range of their studies.[1] They point to the Massachusetts Institute of Tech-

[1] *See,* for instance, *The Complete Scientist,* ed. by SIR PATRICK LINSTEAD (Oxford, 1961).

nology, which has distinguished departments of social studies and by no means neglects literature. But it is not certain even there that the integration of these studies with the technologies has been satisfactorily achieved, and it is certain that this has not been done in our own technical and technological institutions. How can these young men whose minds are on technical studies be persuaded that liberal studies matter to them? Yet if they are not so persuaded will they ever be liberally educated men and women?

Sir Eric Ashby has suggested[1] that to try merely to add a few hours of "liberal studies" to the curriculum in technology is not the right way to go about it. On the contrary we must start where the student's interests are and broaden out from there. This is persuasive up to a point. There is some hope of convincing a young engineer that a workshop is not only a place where the practice of a technology leads to the production of goods, but a human community as well, and that success in production turns in no small measure on the degree to which it is a satisfying community to those who are in it. There is scope here; but there are limits. One cannot be very specific. Take a man who is going to end up (as the fates may know, but he may not) as architect to a firm of brewers. He ought, no doubt, to think of the function of the public house in a community, of the practical needs of the man the brewers put in to run their tied house and of the customers, of the site in relation to the village cricket pitch, of the effect on public taste of good and bad building of public houses, and of the general implications of his directions to make pubs be more modern and at the same time look more antique. But you can't teach him all this directly in his period of training. Somehow it has to be done generally, and in a way that will lead him to think about these things when he does his specialized work.

[1] In *Technology and the Academics* (Macmillan, 1958).

What we need is a thought-out division of responsibility for general education between the schools and the technical or technological colleges. Before we can sketch what such a division of labour might be we must look at the present situation about technical and liberal studies in the schools and in the technical education of young people under the age of eighteen.

We have seen what the general attitude was to technical education in the Public schools up to quite recent times. A decisive influence on the development of publicly maintained secondary schools has been exercised by men themselves educated in the narrow conception of a liberal education inculcated by the Public schools. During this century we have gradually moved from the idea of the publicly maintained schools as places where the poor were given the rudiments of education necessary for rural and industrial workers to the idea of them as places where a liberal education should be given. But at the key points the conception has been that of a modified Arnoldesque liberal education with Aristotelian overtones.

A decisive moment came in the year 1902. Balfour, the Prime Minister, had been persuaded of the need to complement the Act of 1870 with an Act that would set up a system of publicly maintained secondary schools. But at this time we already had a promising beginning of public post-primary education in England: the elementary schools, assisted by the Board of Trade, had grown "tops" that had begun to give us a little of the technical education we needed. Germany, and possibly France, had gone further than we had in technical education, and the former especially was a threatening rival in industry and trade. Now how far Morant, the great power at the Board of Education, was blind to these considerations and hostile to technical education or (as is perhaps more probable) was simply out to kill School Boards that had been exceeding their powers, is a matter of dispute; but in the result he saw to it that, subject of course to a broadening of the curriculum, the publicly maintained secondary schools were to make a continuum with the older grammar schools and be infused with a spirit that was as far as possible a day school echo of the Public boarding school. It is only in recent years, with the marked development of near-vocational studies in the modern and the technical secondary schools and in the local technical colleges, that we have begun to recover from this wrong start. But, as we have seen with the institutions for young people over eighteen, the educational problem remains largely unsolved.

In recent years the Ministry of Education, with much outside support, has tried to correct the crudeness of a straight antithesis between technical and liberal education. It issued a Circular in 1957[1] which spoke of the "liberalizing element" in technical education. This Circular implied that we should not think of liberal education as one thing and of technical education as another, and then add to the latter whatever quantum of the former we thought necessary to constitute a good education. On the contrary, we should consider how far there was a potential liberalizing element in technical education, and then foster it.

We have then to note our starting point. Defined as someone who does not need to work to earn his living and is socially not expected to do so, the English gentleman is dead. This alone invalidates anything like the Aristotelian conception of a liberal education in our society. Secondly, as we have seen, the distinction between supposedly liberal professions and other callings has broken down. Yet is this the whole of the story? Clearly not. We all feel in our bones that there is something still in the original distinction though it has to be reformulated in terms of our own time. This is, quite simply,

[1] Circular 323, May 1957.

that there is a difference between educating and training mere producers and educating civilized men and women.

If this is our aim, how far should we rely on a good general education before technical specialization and how far on broadening the basis of technical and technological studies in the way Sir Eric Ashby suggests?

The idea of a liberal education is linked with the idea of a general education, though it may not be quite the same thing. We may agree that however specialized a man's future work will be, his education should afford him the knowledge and the interests that he needs simply as a human being. Now when there is time this ought not to be difficult. If a young man is going to emerge as a technologist when he has completed his higher education there is no reason why he should not have a good general education first. This is clearly the responsibility of his school, and the great thing to avoid is premature specialization. If he leaves school not only with good mathematics and well grounded in two or three of the sciences, but competent in at least one foreign language, with a knowledge of history and geography and seriously interested in at least one of the arts (literature or music or painting as the case may be) he has the basis for a liberal mental life. His first degree, and especially the first part of it, may be in his professional field, but this should be broadly interpreted, with more than one "subject" of study. If he is going to be an engineer his study of the mathematics and physics necessary to an engineer may well take more time than engineering as such. He should also have time to study something of the economics of engineering and the sociology of the workshop, and he should continue the use of his foreign language for studies in his professional field. It is in his postgraduate work that he should really specialize. The continental technological institutions produce engineers as liberally educated as this, and usually with more than one foreign language. There is no reason why we should not.

Our real difficulty is with the young people who will not go on to higher education and may not even go on to the sixth form. With them we cannot rely on the same range or depth of intellectual interest. There will be some who will be conscious of a fairly well-marked vocational drive, but others who will be content merely with a job of some sort. If we have not yet done very well with these young people in their last year at school still less have we succeeded, in spite of much individual effort, with the liberal studies provided for either full-time or part-time students in further education. Let us consider a very general case.

A high proportion of girls in our secondary modern and comprehensive schools want to become secretaries. What will be the kind of interplay between general education and specific vocational training for such girls, and how far can any of it be thought of as "liberal?" Obviously the years up to fourteen (and soon we can reasonably say fifteen) should be for general education. If after this there is to come something vocational we have to ask a pertinent question: what makes a good secretary? She obviously needs good shorthand and typing, a little training in office skills such as filing and introduction to office machinery, a few hints about "receptionist" duties, and the like. But a good secretary has much more: ability to read through for meaning what she has taken down or typed, and therefore good English and ability to understand whatever kind of business is done in her office. In these days some knowledge of foreign words and phrases is becoming essential, and a bilingual secretary is a great asset in almost any office. If she has a good background of knowledge of history and geography, of our society and how it works, of the sort of things that are discussed in the feature articles of the better newspapers and periodicals, all this will be of direct value to her work. In fact you can't be a first-rate secretary without these things. Of course if one thinks of "commercial subjects" as nothing but training in a few office skills then there is little educational value in them. But a good secretary is one who has had a liberal education, and who is continuing it through her own reading and interests, and if "commercial studies" are taken as a specifically oriented part of this they can be beyond dispute educationally valid. There is no reason at all why such professional education begun in the last year at school should not fuse both with preceding general education and with the studies and skills for the future vocation.

Is this too easy an example? Only perhaps in one respect: that the nature of the work of a future secretary, and therefore of good preparation for it, is more general than that of many callings. There are many other broad categories of occupation that offer similar opportunities: the farm worker, the motor mechanic, the merchant seaman, are examples that spring to mind immediately. But admittedly it becomes more difficult as selection of future jobs becomes more specific. The answer to this is not to let it become too specific too early, certainly not in the school years. This is in the interest of an economy in which there are now bound to be many transfers and changes of occupation in a working life, and in the interest of the individual.

The meaning of the word "liberal" in the phrase "a liberal education" is liberating or freeing. From what? From the tyranny of the routine, the limited, the immediate. In spite of the social changes that have made the phrase out-of-date if we think only of its former contexts, there is this important and fundamental meaning and relevance in it. Without this "value" there cannot be education. There can be only training. We need two things. First (as I have argued) a continuum from the beginning of the last year at school to the end of the first two years in employment and part-time education, so that the fusion between general education and vocational education and training is felt by a boy or girl to be real. And secondly a much more imaginative exploration of the possibilities of liberalizing through technical education itself.

3. Moral Values in Education

The two value problems we have discussed are not easy ones. We are, however, reasonably clear in our minds as to what we mean by intellectual values and we know the general nature of our obligation to them. We are less clear about the concept of a liberal education and its actual and possible relationship with technical teaching, but if we look at the problem as it has developed in successive stages of society and analyse the concept till we have separated out the essential from the accidental meanings, we can at least define the nature of our task. But if we set out to discuss moral values and education we soon find that we are in more difficult territory. The first weapon in the philosopher's armoury, the question: "What does the concept mean?", will have its uses; but heavier artillery will be needed. We have to consider the relationship, in concept and in practice, between moral values and other things, such as religious beliefs. We confront an actual contemporary situation in which there is great confusion: the schools are frequently upbraided for not doing more to instil sound moral values in the young, yet what "sound moral values" are, society does not say, though vociferous and mutually contradictory sections of it do. Our student teachers have it impressed upon them that this subject is of great importance but as something to be systematically studied in its own right it virtually does not exist in our training colleges. In the world outside the parents blame the teachers, the teachers blame the parents, and both blame the "mass media," easy money, the falling off in church attendance or half a dozen other things. Probably no two people agree, in any case, as to the degree to which the schools are failing in moral education, if they are.

Here I can of course attempt nothing systematic. I should not be competent to marshal a discussion in terms of ethical theory, but like all educationists I have been forced to think about the question. There are some propositions that seem to me almost self-evident, and on which we are not yet acting, and these I should like to formulate with some indication of their policy implications.

The first proposition is so easy to state that it looks like a truism, but as soon as one begins to elaborate upon it one is in trouble. The statement is simply that the schools do have a duty in the moral education of the young. There would be few people who would deny this, but equally there would be many who would be on their guard as soon as they heard it said. It is the sort of thing that has been said rather often by dictators and bigots, and the teacher wants to say something additional immediately, that we mustn't suppose that outward conformity to conventional standards is the same thing as being a moral person, that if we try to secure inner acceptance by anything like brainwashing we are doing violence to the young, and so on. The teacher has his own position to consider too. He will be blamed for not exercising a good moral influence, yet some moral questions are matters of controversy and he must not abuse his trust by making propaganda for views that may be his own but not those of others. But let us leave these not unimportant footnotes. There can be no doubt that schools are an agency in the transmission of the norms of a society to the next generation and that among these norms are those pertaining to moral conduct.

This very formulation suggests a static society, as ours is not. It is in such a society that the situation may be seen at its simplest. There is no disagreement as to what the norms of conduct should be. The duty of the teacher is to transmit them to the young, so that they master any formal codes and so "interiorize" the values that they become matters of conscience. Static societies of the past have often been like this until they have been exposed to contact with societies having different norms. Commonly the moral codes of such a society have had religious beliefs as their sanction, and although there may have been religious and moral backsliders no one has dared question either the religious beliefs or the moral norms as such. There is hardly any such society in the world now, certainly not our own. We have to think out our problems of moral education against a background of rapid social, intellectual and religious change.

This leads me to a second statement that also, though with different degrees of emphasis, will command general assent, and which again has difficult implications. We are now a multi-belief society. In England today, judging by the not unreasonable test of fairly regular church attendance, there is a minority of active Christians; how large or small a minority is a matter on which people would disagree, but it is certainly a minority whereas it was a majority a hundred years ago. There is also a minority, a smaller one though a growing one, which more or less consciously rejects traditional religious beliefs and religious observances. In between there is a very large group of people who avail themselves of religious rituals for special occasions like weddings and funerals, who would probably say "I suppose so" if asked if they believed in a God, but whose daily conduct is not, so far as one can tell, influenced by any active religious belief. It would certainly seem to be a valid inference from this state of affairs that we could not rely on religious warrant for moral education for the school population as a whole. Too many of the young come from homes where such sanctions are not upheld. (Perhaps in parenthesis I had better deal with an obvious comment, that "sanction" may be an unfair word since the best religious moral teachers do not say: "This is morally right because God tells you to do it," but: "what is morally right is what God approves your doing." The emphasis in schools is, one suspects, more on the former sequence than the latter in the period of Religious Instruction, but the point about the latter is that of course it admits that a sense of what is morally right may be instilled without a logically prior belief in a God.)

Now although the moral influence of a school depends upon the teaching in many subjects, and above all on the general tone set apart from what is formally taught, the period of Religious Instruction and to some degree the morning religious assembly are the only designated occasions where there can be systematic moral teaching and discussion; and there would be a wide agreement that moral education relying on these means is not reaching a considerable body of the young. In face of this situation some people, like a former Minister of Education, call for a more determined attempt in schools and training colleges to inculcate "absolute" values through religious belief, an attempt which one would have thought could not now have major success, and if it did could do so only by offending the parents who are not religious (except for those who think religion good for children but unnecessary for themselves, a precarious position that child logic often penetrates). Other people would have the period of Religious Instruction become essentially one for moral education within a religious framework. This is also logically precarious, for although religions have their closely associated moral codes and outlooks, religion and morals are not identical any more than theology and ethics are. And the attempt to keep the religious framework but to do something different leads to a forcing that is sometimes rather absurd. ("What can Amos tell us about Rachmanism?" as I saw on one draft syllabus).

This actual situation, and the doubtful logic of the positions taken to meet it, are gradually making people realize that we must recognize a need that is new, at least in the form it takes. It was this that Lord Brain had in mind when he said in his Presidential Address to the British Association for the Advancement of Science in 1964, that education must concern itself with the whole man, and therefore with behaviour, and went on: "Here it must largely reflect the views and standards of society; and one of our needs as a society, now predominantly secular, is to develop a code of social responsibility which can form an integral part of education." If we now recognize this need we have two difficult questions to face. First, how do we conceive of moral values in relation to religious beliefs? And secondly, can we reasonably hope to agree as moral educationists even though we differ in religion or philosophy?

For a religious person moral standards will seem to be integrated with his beliefs. To take the most familiar traditional example, the Ten Commandments for him will have been given by God. For the person standing outside this framework of religious beliefs it will seem that this is merely the form that the moral injunctions took and that without the beliefs there would still have been need and justification for something of the sort. Now for working purposes, though not for theoretical discussion, these two positions are by no means impossible to reconcile. If the religious person is speaking with some one that supposed divine law leaves unimpressed, he resorts to arguments from natural law, and except where some alleged divine law conflicts with what the humanist alleges is demanded by human experience, the two positions are close enough to permit of rational discussion and, in a society of given traditions and modes, of a great deal of agreement. What is needed is simply to persuade moralists who for themselves feel religious beliefs to be the basis of their morality, to discuss with those who do not *as if* sound moral standards could be defended in terms of our experience of what is right and good. This surely ought not to be all that difficult.

Dr. A. L. Rowse, in his book *The Use of History*,[1] quoted the late Professor Stebbing (who was what we now would call a "humanist") as follows—

> It is an illusion to find the value of our lives here and now in a life to come; it is an illusion to suppose that nothing is worth while for me unless I live forever; it is an illusion to suppose that there is no uncompensated loss, no sacrifice that is without requital, no grief that is unassuaged. But it is also no illusion but uncontested fact that here and now we know that hatred, cruelty, intolerance, and indifference to human misery are evil; that love, kindliness, tolerance, forgiveness, and truth are good, so unquestionably good that we do not need God or heaven to assure us of their worth.

Rowse agrees, adding that these values emerge from and rest upon the positive experience of man in history.

Now persons with religious beliefs might not be at ease with the first sentence in this passage, and might be doubtful of the last phrase in the second. But they must agree with the main point: that human experience tells us that the qualities Miss Stebbing says are good are indeed good, and those she says are bad are indeed bad. This is so obvious that it would seem to be quite uncontroversial. And it is equally obvious that it can be the basis, and the only practical basis, for agreed moral education in a society where there are many religious beliefs and also people with none. It is odd that we cannot come together and act upon this.

Here, perhaps paradoxically, I am suggesting that we ought to ask a few questions that would be prompted by a little philosophical reading, but not too many. At the present time those who are agonizing over what they feel to be the low standards of moral education and are repeating dogmatic

[1] Hodder and Stoughton, 1946; p. 154.

insistences to which fewer and fewer people listen, ought to ask a few basic questions as to the relation between theology and ethics, between religious and moral education. Nobody is going to suggest that further discussion as to the sources of our values, whether social or supernatural, is unimportant; but I do suggest that if we let this dominate us too much in our working relationships in a multi-belief society we shall fight each other in a field where we might honestly collaborate. In our society the Hobbes position would be intolerable; the thesis that the only way to prevent us from getting at each other's throats is for some sovereign authority to dictate what we shall all believe. The Locke position, favouring tolerance and disposition to work together in committee for something practical we can agree on even though ultimately we might disagree, lacks the attraction of intellectual incisiveness but is infinitely preferable in practice. It is, above all, likely to work with us because this habit has become inbred in us in the last three centuries and commends itself to most of us as good sense.[1]

This question might profitably be considered in another context, that of the general development of our educational theory. In fact what we need is an extension to the field of moral education of the attitudes we have increasingly adopted in education generally.

Education is concerned with bringing up the young. But bringing them up to be what? To be adult men and women, no doubt. But what kind of adult men and women? Whether we are teachers, parents or members of the general public the whole point of what we are doing in education depends on our answer to that question. The question really breaks down into two. What is the nature of Man (or, if you prefer, of

[1] Perhaps I might refer to an article in which I developed this argument: Can Educationists Agree while Philosophers Differ? (*Adult Education*, December, 1947).

men and women)? What ought Man (or men and women) to be like?

In the answers that have been given to these questions one may distinguish two broad streams of thought.[1] There are answers that posit some "essential" nature of Man. Such answers are associated with a system of Absolute Values, ultimately apprehended as Truth revealed from sources beyond phenomenal Nature. Plato gave answers of this kind. Those who approach education from the standpoint of certain Christian dogmas are in the same general category. Secondly, there are answers that base themselves on the observation of human beings and their development from birth onwards, and on values seen as derived from human experience, individual and collective. This approach is naturally congenial to humanists; but—and this is my point here—it has increasingly been adopted for working purposes by those whose ultimate allegiance would be to the first position.

The "child-centred" view of education is patently inadequate (Rousseau, one of the traditional great names in the history of its development, was just plain silly about social and moral education, supposing that it could and should be postponed till a child was virtually a young man); but it was historically liberating. It protested against bringing up the young to some preordained pattern and treating them as if they were merely small adults. It encouraged, on the contrary, finding out what children actually were like and how they did develop; and with the establishment of psychology as a recognized study this became immensely significant and has modified our whole educational practice. This has meant a great shift of emphasis from the absolute to the relative, from the dogmatic to the observational. It is indeed difficult to

[1] For a systematic review of these two tendencies *see* SUCHODOLSKI, *La Pédagogie et les Grands Courants Philosophiques* (Paris, Editions du Scarabée, 1960).

recall now that only a century ago all children were brought up on the assumption that their nature was founded in "original sin" and that the great object of education must be to save them from the consequences of this. Preconceived theories of human—and child—nature now govern our educational practices much less, real knowledge and genuine insight govern them much more.

What was left out of the more naïve versions of "child-centred" education was the understanding that we must not merely liberate the child's own personality but also consider the social norms in accordance with which we educate him as a member of society. We wish him to become a moral person, that is to say a being capable of making responsible moral choices. This means that while we indeed observe how the young do develop, and while we do respect their personalities, we have to make them aware of the values necessary for a good individual and social life, including the capacity to consider alternative or conflicting values responsibly.

A moral value is a general principle of behaviour, not a particular decision that might flow from the conscious recognition of a value. Believing or not believing in the permissibility of divorce does not constitute a value. Our views about this flow from values. Some may say that marriage is only true marriage if it is accompanied by solemn vows and that to break these vows is to offend against the sanctity of undertakings freely entered into in the sight of God, and that to respect this is more important than ending an unhappy relationship. Others will say that less suffering may be caused if very unsatisfactory marriages are ended. They are saying that the value of so acting as to produce the greatest happiness (or the least unhappiness) for those concerned is greater than the value of maintaining, in perpetuity and irrespective of circumstances and the desires of both parties, a contract entered into earlier.

Now both these arguments rest on moral considerations, though on different ones. What is very intolerant is to suggest that one is "moral" and the other "immoral." In any case the majority of people will no longer accept that as closing the argument. They want to discuss the respective weight they should give to the two moral values invoked. The difference is that the defenders of the former normally invoke a religious sanction, whereas the defenders of the latter do not. Now even though the short and sufficient answer to those who would base the whole of moral education on religous beliefs is that this will not work in a multi-belief society, most people will wish to think where they do stand in this matter.

It would be reasonable to say that in the short run, for those who have a firm system of religious beliefs, those beliefs may act as a reinforcing agent for the moral code associated with the beliefs. But this cuts both ways. The moral code may include some practices that, on moral grounds, ought to be abandoned. The simplest way to make this clear to persons of one religion (who find it hard to believe that anything in their moral code could need revision) is to draw their attention to practices in the codes of other religions that they find repellent. Thus, although there were some English administrators who doubted whether we should interfere with the practice of *suttee* in India in the early nineteenth century, since this would be interfering with a practice sanctioned by religion, majority opinion found the burning of widows when a man died an intolerable practice, and we decided (as none now would doubt, rightly) to stamp it out. In the end, the appeal to human experience usually succeeds, but after a time lag in which there is often immense human suffering. However, it is also probable that an individual gains strength from his religious affiliations for minority moral standards that may be good. Quakers, for instance, undoubtedly gain strength in this way for the general predisposition to non-violence, though how far this is a strength of a credal kind and how far a strength coming from a group solidarity of responsible like-minded persons might be questioned.

On this matter there is, however, a certain amount of nonsense talked. I have even heard it said that, if we did not believe in a God who told us not to, we should steal from the counter at Woolworth's. We do not steal from the counter at Woolworth's because we have built into us (and reinforced by a judicious knowledge of possible penalties) a social standard that makes us know that this would be wrong. There is not the slightest evidence that the tendency to pilfer is greater among the children of unbelievers than among the children of believers. A firmly religious person, moreover, would have no more difficulty than a humanist in explaining, in terms of human experience alone, why such behaviour is anti-social and morally wrong.

This leads us back to the main stream of the argument. Our general educational theory familiarizes us more and more with the idea that we should study how the young do develop, and we are by no means without knowledge as to how they develop as social and moral beings. This should be the ground-work for our educational practice. But that does not answer our question: develop into what? For here we have varying possibilities. We have seen that as we are now a multi-belief society we need an answer to this question that commands general support and that can rest (must rest for those who are not actively religious, may rest for those who are) on the values we derive from human experience. The crucial question now is: whatever our differing explanations of the sources of our moral values, can we agree enough in practice on what is right conduct to give us coherence in our moral educational aims?

Setting aside certain particular questions (such as divorce, which I have already instanced), and on which discussion in the upper ranges of a school can itself be educationally valid, I would say that we can, and much more than has been generally recognized so far. We should all subscribe to the values expressed by Susan Stebbing to begin with. But, beyond this, there is a surprising consensus in our society as to what does constitute good conduct, as to what makes a "decent" man or woman. We are a long-settled community in this country and have evolved almost a code to which most of us instinctively subscribe. It is difficult not to run to clichés, but the clichés stand for something. The appeal to "fair play," for instance, if legitimately made is almost always effective with us. The belief in letting every man have and express his own opinion, short of violence or the threat of it, is now inbred in us. The belief that if you have individual rights you nevertheless also have social responsibilities has worked itself out with us in a thousand practical ways. There are areas, it is true, of uncertainty. Sexual morals are clearly in transition, yet even here no one believes in irresponsible conduct or in not respecting other people as persons. The biggest gap between what the schools try to inculcate and what society seems to honour is in the reputability of mere acquisitiveness, and here it must be said that the schools cannot go much further than they have in inculcating better values until society takes itself in hand. But by and large there is a basis for agreed action in education of which we have not taken advantage because we have not envisaged moral education as something in its own right, not necessarily instead of religious education (that is a different question, into which I am not going here) but not vainly dependent upon it as it is now.

How is this to be translated into school terms? The first thing to recognize is that there is a whole range of moral questions in which young people are intensely interested, on condition that the discussion is open and not dogmatically closed in advance. It would be a poor teacher who could not hold the attention of a normal class, due to leave school in one more year, in systematic discussion of a multitude of problems that they know concern them. They are intensely interested in how they are going to conduct themselves in the world outside, in the factory, the shop, the office, the cinema, the dance hall, the club and the street; and not least in the home, at a moment when relations between parents and their young adult children are bound to raise questions. They are of course interested in how young men are going to conduct themselves with girls, and vice versa, and the relation of this to something more permanent, and not least to marriage and children. They are interested in clothes, make-up, smoking, drinking, and all the other things that they see as self-expression and the "unco guid" as on the edge of delinquency. They are interested in delinquency itself. They are interested in social questions that have a moral basis, in capital punishment and race relations, for instance. The list is indeed almost inexhaustible. But— and this is an all-important but—they want to talk about these things (and they sometimes hardly know how) in an "open," not a closed, setting. They indeed will talk with adults about them, if these have something to contribute on these terms. This does not mean without personal attitudes, or even without convictions. But it does mean without commandments that virtually close the discussion before it has begun.

This means one thing in terms of when and where it is done. It means outside, not inside, "R.I." Maybe a period in the time-table labelled "Ethics" would not be right. I am not sure. Certainly towards the upper end of the school age there should be periods specially set aside for such systematic and structured discussions. And there should be quite specific preparation for it in the teacher training colleges. It is not every teacher who could handle this, and even those who potentially can will welcome intelligent help and preparation for it. It may be more difficult to work for moral responsibility and sensitiveness without the rigid commandments. But that now is the only way for the generality of our young people. And it might produce finer human beings.

We are a long way yet from even understanding the need for a new start. Sixty years ago now Durkheim was calling for something of the same kind in France. His call did not fall entirely on deaf ears. To some extent at least the *Instituteur* has stood in every French village for certain values, values that were different from those of the *ancien régime* and which contributed decisively to the moral fibre of the Third Republic. It is worth recalling Durkheim's words, for they are not without significance for our own situation in this country now—

> The educational problem presents itself to us in a specially urgent way. In saying this I have been thinking especially of our system of moral education, which, as you see, needs to be very largely rebuilt in its main constituents. We can no longer make use of the traditional system, which, moreover, has for long only kept itself going by a miracle of balance, by the force of habit. For a long time now it has not rested on a solid enough basis; for a long time it has not rested on beliefs strong enough to enable it effectively to discharge its functions. But to replace it usefully it is not enough to tear off the labels. It will not do to take away a few tags, at the risk moreover of taking away at the same time substantial realities. We have to go forward to a recasting of our educational techniques.[1]

4. *Community Values in Education*

Through all the argument of this book there has been running the thread of one question, and in this concluding section I should like to put it explicitly. Is our education in this country doing as much as it should to prepare us to be members of one community? One might say, in the biblical phrase,

[1] EMILE DURKHEIM, *La Morale Laique* (*L'Education Morale*).

to be "members one of another." Or if that is too pious, to think of ourselves as all members of one team. Or if that is too corny, simply to feel ourselves one society with differences that add to the interest of living in it but without divisions that impoverish its life.

It is normal for a national society to look on its schools as very important agents for inculcating a national consciousness, and this is held without question to be a good thing. It also considers the schools as important agents for inducing general approval of the kind of society it has. But the English situation is paradoxical. We seem to want to be both united as a nation and divided as a society, and our educational arrangements reflect this double aim. From Eton, with its playing fields on which the Battle of Waterloo was won, to the Council schools and their successors where the civilian Battle of London was won, we all "believe in England." But do Eton and its like on the one hand, and the publicly maintained schools on the other, do more in fact to unite or to divide us? Two broad groups of Englishmen are sent to school in two different kinds of establishment, and we hardly ever talk to those from a different circle in any intimate way after that.

This puzzles and perplexes the visitor. Let me quote from Mr. V. S. Naipaul, the distinguished West Indian novelist. He said recently in the *Evening Standard*[1]—

No country with a population of 50 million is as united as England is. Yet, within this unity, class leads to social impoverishment. It limits communication between groups and replaces it by the spirit of service, the joke English attribute which yet mitigates the jungle ethics which this odd opportunist, capitalist welfare state always threatens. The spirit of service, issuing out of class, makes for further stability. In some countries everything conspires to maintain chaos. In England everything conspires to maintain calm. But service is not a true substitute for communication. Class

[1] September 15th, 1964.

imprisons. And as cities grow, it imprisons more securely. It divides more minutely as skills grow more specialized. Life grows steadily less communal.

Most people, I think, would recognize this as a pretty fair and accurate description of us.

But perhaps this really is the kind of society most people in this country want. They would say: "Yes, we are all English, but we don't want to have more than a small social circle, with people of our own kind, which means of roughly our own level of income. This does not mean that we are rude to other people or won't pass the time of day with them when occasion offers, nor does it mean that we shall not feel a sense of obligation if they are in need of help. It means only that our social intercourse is with our own social sort. If the people in such a circle of friends can all afford much the same sort of pleasures it saves embarrassment all round. Isn't this, after all, what most people want?"

This of course is not quite an answer. We all know people who keep themselves very much to themselves, hardly vary the routine of sleep and work and eating, with a few virtually solitary pleasures; and they may say that is the way they would prefer to live. But that does not prevent our saying of such a person: "it is a pity he (or she) has lived such a narrow life." This is not a question of temperament. Some people are more reserved by nature, others more gregarious, and every man has the right to be which he pleases. Nor are we discussing the right to certain group intimacies; we may be justly annoyed if some stranger insists on inflicting his company on a group of close friends talking together about matters that interest them but not everybody who might decide to join them. In English society we respect privacies of this kind, and there is nothing wrong with that. The question before us is a different one, whether a contrived social structuring, reinforced by educational segregation, is not depriving our society of a vitality and a wider enjoyment that it might otherwise have. This certainly goes beyond mere matters of personal taste and temperament.

First, even in the matter of manners, there is an appeal to common experience. Most English people who do have the chance of a freer human range seem, so long as it is within limits of good manners, to enjoy it. Everybody who remembers the last war also remembers the strange pleasure, almost the elation, that people felt when they found themselves talking in the air raid shelter with other people to whom ordinarily they would not have dreamed of talking. Some English people find a similar sense of release when they visit Commonwealth countries or the United States.

This is not a question of mere *bonhomie*. It is one of a shared sense of living in a common society. Those who dislike the artificial barriers that we put up are not to be dismissed as sentimentalists. They are raising a question that concerns the quality of our living. Once years ago, in a dingy Labour Hall, I saw on the wall the words: "Fellowship is life; and lack of fellowship is death. William Morris." That may sound sentimental, because the word "fellowship" is itself too Morrissy now and perhaps always was a little self-conscious. But Morris, though none would have been more appalled than he by the drabness of that place, was right. There is of course a sentimentality of cheeriness which itself can be quite dreadful. But it is still true that the person who is so conditioned that he can only enjoy a *de luxe* holiday, and cannot possibly bring himself to set out walking and sleep where he finds a bed, is missing something. The person who feels socially uncomfortable unless he can travel first-class on a train, even if it is almost empty, has lost a faculty. There are many things that as individuals we do not have in common with everybody we may meet; but the man who cannot share a sense of regret or delight in the things we do have in common, except within the confines of his own little group, is surely missing a great deal. This level of living is surely not to be ignored. Do we really wish to breed people who go through the fields in their status-conscious gloves, "missing so much and so much?"

But the important considerations go deeper. Shelley was right when he argued in *The Defence of Poetry* that the sympathetic imagination is the heart of morality. Certainly, the classes and social groups in England are not consciously cruel to each other, and they do have a sense of service. But, as Mr. Raymond Williams argued towards the end of his book on *Culture and Society*,[1] a sense of service is not the same thing as a sense of community. In a good community there is great scope for individual differences, but there is also a strong sense of shared experience. If our schools induce or reinforce structural differences which inhibit this too much then there will be a deprivation in our society. Many foreign observers, like Mr. Naipaul, feel that we are so depriving ourselves, and he would no doubt agree that our educational arrangements have a good deal to do with the result.

This brings us back to the questions we raised in the introductory chapter. Whatever society and whatever educational system we may favour, we must recognize that the question of the social effect of our education is a legitimate and a very important question. Perhaps it is arguable whether we are very serious when we describe ourselves as a democracy, except in the sense that we do not want a political dictatorship. If we do include social ideas of equality in that concept then it is hard to believe that we can accept with equanimity the present divisive social effects of our school systems. Sweden also calls itself a democracy and we noted that they take this kind of consideration more seriously than we do. There is a clear social view behind the current school reforms there (and they have no "private sector"!). The Chief Inspector of

[1] Chatto and Windus, 1958.

Schools, Mr. Jonas Orring, says in his book *Comprehensive School and Continuation Schools in Sweden*[1]—

> Social and human factors are just as important for the individual and society in the world of today and tomorrow as are intellectual ones. The greatest of current problems is the inability of people to live and work happily together—not to attain new and greater intellectual performance. But the ability to work and live together in harmony is only slightly developed by one-sided intellectual training. It is fostered in practical forms by work, and presumes a common fund of education and experience. Questions of prestige and evaluation should not be allowed to enter the world of the school until some social resistance to them has been created.

We would do well to note the balance of this. The argument is not for an ignoring of differences in ability and quality, but for a common social experience first, and the Swedish reformed structure will be that of a common school to the age of fifteen or sixteen with differentiation thereafter. Nor, it should be added, would any one be likely to accuse Swedish society of lacking respect for the intellectual values.

This is what is to be understood by a common culture. Not "admass" indeed, but a sufficiency of common experience, above all of that richly formative sort that comes from mixing with all sorts of boys and girls when one is young, to enable the *élites* (in the sense not of power groups but of especially gifted people) to feel that they are *élites* within general society, not outside it, and to enable the generality of men and women to feel that the *élites* are part of their society also. It is quite possible that the children in Mrs. Marshall's village school in Cambridgeshire have now gone very different ways. The scientist's child and the professor's child, with their home backing, may be university teachers or research workers— or they may be running a garage. One or two of the children may have got to the university, three or four to the grammar

[1] Kungl. Ecklesiastikdepartementet, Stockholm, 1962 (pp. 31, 32).

school. But I suspect that few if any would regret that they had all been to the village school. There *was* something wrong with the life of the village, with the farmers and their wives being unwilling to let their children be contaminated by going to school with the labourers' children, though the teaching was good enough for the academics. They both lost something, the labourers' and the farmers' children.

The Times was wrong to suggest that discussions such as this are not in the strict sense educational at all. They are the essence of it. The defence of the Public schools we heard was not adequate, because it dodged this criticism. The attack on those who favoured comprehenseive schools for social reasons was also more than a little out of court, though when all the relevant factors are taken into account there may well be more to be said (even by those, like myself, who vastly prefer the full comprehensive school to the tripartite structure from the age of eleven plus) for a common school to fifteen and differentiated education thereafter. As for Mrs. Smith-James, of 5 Acacia Avenue, she was assuredly not wrong in wanting her Elizabeth and Robin to speak well and have good manners (though these are not always what suburbia supposes). And if in her case the alternative was a school like those described by Dr. Mays, labouring under the greatest handicaps, she may have been right in the interests of her own young. But there was one thought that clearly had never entered her mind: that even though they thereby gained a little privileged standing, it might in the broader sense be a social *dis*advantage for her children to go to a socially separate school. When that possibility comes home to people in England, we shall have made some progress towards being a social democracy.

FOR FURTHER READING

THIS is not a systematic bibliography, but a list of books (some of which have been mentioned in the text) for readers who may wish to carry further the study of education and contemporary society in the way suggested in this book. It is in four sections, corresponding to the four sections of Part I, with a fifth section of books about contemporary educational problems. The headings (sociological, philosophical, etc.) should be considered as approximate rather than as academically strict; and some books might well appear under more than one of these headings.

A. *Sociological*

HALSEY, A. H., FLOUD, JEAN and ANDERSON, C. A., *Education, Economy and Society* (Free Press, Glencoe, 1961). A voluminous reader in the whole subject of the sociology of education.

OTTAWAY, A. K. C., *Education and Society* (Routledge & Kegan Paul, 1953). A good general introduction to the subject.

Among studies of the social structure of England, either in general or with special reference to education, the following may be noted—

CARR-SAUNDERS, A. M., JONES, D. and MOSER, C. A., *Social Conditions in England and Wales* (Oxford, Clarendon Press, 1958). A statistical and factual summary of English social conditions.

COLE, G. D. H., *Studies in Class Structure* (Routledge & Kegan Paul, 1955). This has a section on *Elites* in British Society, with a sub-section on the educational factors.

FLOUD, JEAN (ed.) HALSEY, A. H. and MARTIN, F. M., *Social Class and Educational Opportunity* (Heinemann, 1956).

GLASS, DAVID (ed.), *Social Mobility in Britain* (Routledge & Kegan Paul, 1954).

PEAR, T. H., *English Social Differences* (Allen & Unwin, 1955). This also has an educational section.

ZWEIG, F., *The Student in the Age of Anxiety* (Heinemann, 1963). A study, based on questionnaires and interviews, of students at Oxford and Manchester, has a good deal of socially interesting material.

On the home and neighbourhood background of education the following may be noted—

DOUGLAS, J. W. B., *The Home and the School* (McGibbon & Kee, 1964).

FLETCHER, R., *The Family* (Penguin Books, 1962).

MARSHALL, SYBIL, *An Experiment in Education* (Cambridge, 1963). This is primarily an account of education through the arts in a Cambridgeshire village school, but it has incidental social observations of some interest.

MAYS, J. B., *Education and the Urban Child* (Liverpool, 1962).

"MISS READ", *Village School* (Michael Joseph, 1956).

REEVES, MARJORIE, *Growing Up in a Modern Society* (Univ. of London Press, 1946).

Among books that discuss, in different ways, the problem of the education of *élites* in relation to general society, and of minority culture in relation to the culture of the community, the following may be noted—

ARNOLD, MATTHEW, *Culture and Anarchy* (C.U.P. 1932). A classic, possibly too insistently a "set book," but still well worth reading.

BOTTOMORE, T. B., *Elites and Society* (Watts, 1964).

ELIOT, T. S., *Notes towards the Definition of Culture* (Faber, 1948).

HALSEY, A. H. (ed.), *Ability and Educational Opportunity* (O.E.C.D., Paris, 1961).

HUGHES, H. STUART, *Consciousness and Society* (Vintage Books, New York, 1961). A study of the problem of *élites* as seen by Italian, German and French thinkers, 1890–1930.

WILLIAMS, RAYMOND, *Culture and Society* (Chatto & Windus, 1958).

WILLIAMS, RAYMOND, *The Long Revolution* (Chatto & Windus, 1961).

YOUNG, MICHAEL, *The Rise of the Meritocracy* (Thames & Hudson, 1958).

Reference has also been made in the text to the interesting essays by—

FLOUD, JEAN, *Sociology and Education* (Sociology Review Monograph No. 4, Keele, 1961).

MADGE, CHARLES, *Elements of Social Eidos* (Faber, 1964).

Another book that discusses some of the questions considered by Professor Madge is—

BANTOCK, G. H., *Education in an Industrial Society* (Faber, 1963).

Among sociologists who are of importance in the particular context of this book three especially may be mentioned: Durkheim and Max Weber (the work of neither of these is easily or completely accessible in English) and Karl Mannheim.

Reference may be made to the following—

DURKHEIM, EMILE, *Education and Society*, trans. S. D. Fox (Free Press, Glencoe, 1956).

DURKHEIM, EMILE, *Moral Education*, trans. S. D. Fox (Free Press, Glencoe, 1961).

GERTH, H. G. and MILLS, C. WRIGHT, *From Max Weber* (O.U.P., 1946).

WEBER, MAX., *Basic Concepts in Sociology*, trans. H. P. Secker (New York, Citadel Press, 1962).

MANNHEIM, KARL, *Man and Society* (Kegan Paul, 1940).

MANNHEIM, KARL, *Diagnosis of our Time* (Kegan Paul, 1943).

MANNHEIM KARL, *Essays in the Sociology of Culture* (Kegan Paul, 1956).

For an evaluation of Mannheim, see—

FLOUD, JEAN, "Karl Mannheim" in *The Function of Teaching* (ed. A. V. Judges) (Faber, 1959).

HOYLE, ERIC, *The Elite Concept in Karl Mannheim's Sociology of Education* (Sociological Review, Keele, March, 1964).

B. *Psychological*

Books bearing on genetic and environmental factors in ability and ways in which abilities may be measured—

FURNEAUX, W. D., *The Chosen Few* (O.U.P. 1961). A discussion of selection problems by a writer who gives more weight to genetic factors.

HEIM, ALICE, *The Appraisal of Intelligence* (Methuen 1964).

NATIONAL FOUNDATION FOR EDUCATIONAL RESEARCH, *Procedures for the Allocation of Pupils in Secondary Education* (1963).

VERNON, P. E., *Intelligence and Attainment Tests* (Univ. of London Press, 1960).

VERNON, P. E.,Evidence to the Robbins Committee in *The Sociological Review*, No. 7 (ed. Halmos, Keele, 1963). This paper attacks the idea of a genetically fixed pool of ability.

WISEMAN, STEPHEN, *Education and Environment* (Manchester U.P., 1964). Attempts a balanced assessment between genetic and environmental factors.

Among the many works of social psychology the following may be noted as relevant to the point of view of this book—

BANDURA, A. and WALTERS R. H., *Social Learning and Personality Development* (Holt, Rinehart & Winston, 1963). An important corrective book, reasserting the social factor in learning.

ERIKSON, ERIK, *Childhood and Society* (Imago Pub. Co. n.d. and Norton, New York, 1950). A largely psychoanalytic approach to the problem.

FLEMING, C. M., *The Social Psychology of Education* (Kegan Paul, 1944). A review of the subject up to the time of publication.

WALL, W. D., *Child of our Times* (National Children's Home, 1962). A stimulating essay in social psychology related to the broad pattern of contemporary life.

Reference should also be made to the *Year Book of Education*, **1962**, of the London University Institute of Education and Teachers College, Columbia (Evans Bros. and World Book Co.). It contains numerous articles bearing on the question of the "pool of ability."

C. *Philosophical*

The best exposition of the view that we must first decide what kind of society we want and then educate the young for it is still Plato's.

PLATO, *The Republic*, trans. F. M. Cornford (O.U.P., 1941) or H. D. P. Lee (Penguin Books, 1955).

The objections to this concept of a "closed" society are cogently set out in—

POPPER, KARL, *The Open Society and its Enemies*, Vol. I (Routledge, 1945).

Useful general commentaries—
CASTLE, E. B., *Ancient Education and Today* (Penguin Books, 1961).
CROSSMAN, R. H. S., *Plato Today* (Allen & Unwin, 2nd edn., 1959).

Among philosophers who have written about education and have been markedly influenced by the society in which they have written one must mention at least Locke, Rousseau and Dewey. Convenient texts are—
BOYD, WILLIAM, *Emile for Today* (Heinemann, 1956).
DEWEY, JOHN, *Experience and Education* (New York, Macmillan, 1951).
DEWEY, JOHN, *Democracy and Education* (New York, Macmillan, 1955).
DWORKIN, M. S., *Dewey on Education* (Teachers College, Columbia, 1959).
GAY, PETER, *John Locke on Education* (Teachers College, Columbia, 1964).
LOCKE, JOHN, *Some Thoughts concerning Education*, ed. F. W. Garforth (Heinemann, 1964).
ROUSSEAU, J.-J., *Emile* (Dent, Everyman Edn.).

For discussion among educationists in this country of "individualist" and "social" views of education see—
NUNN, PERCY, *Education: Its Data and First Principles* (Arnold, 3rd edn., 1945).
CLARKE, FRED, *Education and Social Change* (Sheldon Press, 1940).
CLARKE, FRED, *Freedom in the Educative Society* (Univ. of London Press, 1948).
Two books by philosophers of this century that should certainly be read are—
RUSSELL, BERTRAND, *On Education* (Allen & Unwin, 1926).
WHITEHEAD, A. N., *Aims of Education* (Benn, 1962).

A book that may perhaps best be described as that of a moralist is—
TAWNEY, R. H., *Equality* (Allen & Unwin, 4th edn., 1962).

Among recent books by ethical or social philosophers, many of them concerned with the question of "values" and with the clarification of concepts in discussing them, the following should be noted—

BENN, S. L. and PETERS, R. S., *Social Principles and the Democratic State* (Allen & Unwin, 1959).

KÖHLER, W., *The Place of Value in a World of Facts* (Kegan Paul, & New York, Liveright, 1938).

MYRDAL, GUNNAR, *Value in Social Theory*, ed. Paul Streeten (Routledge & Kegan Paul, 1958). A somewhat unorthodox view.

O'CONNOR, D. J., *An Introduction to the Philosophy of Education* (Routledge, 1957).

PETERS, R. S., *Authority, Responsibility and Education* (Allen & Unwin, 1959).

REID, L. A., *Philosophy and Education* (Heinemann, 1962).

ROBINSON, RICHARD, *An Atheist's Values* (O.U.P., 1964).

RUNCIMAN, W. G., *Social Science and Political Theory* (C.U.P., 1963).

SCHEFFLER, ISRAEL, *The Language of Education* (Oxford, Blackwell, 1960).

STEVENSON, CHAS. L., *Ethics and Language* (Yale U.P., 1945).

STEVENSON, CHAS. L., *Facts and Values* (Yale U.P., 1963).

TOULMIN, STEPHEN, *The Place of Reason in Ethics* (C.U.P., 1958).

WILSON, JOHN, *Language and the Pursuit of Truth* (C.U.P., 1956).

WILSON, JOHN, *Thinking with Concepts* (C.U.P., 1963).

D. *Comparative*

BENEDICT, RUTH, *Patterns of Culture* (Houghton Mifflin, New York; Routledge, 1935). A book that, with the publications of Malinovski, and the continuing influence of Frazer's *Golden Bough*, gave a decisive impulse to the "relativist" idea of cultural and moral values.

HANS, NICHOLAS, *Comparative Education* (Routledge, 3rd. edn, 1958).

KING, EDMUND, *World Perspectives in Education* (Methuen, 1962).

KING, EDMUND, *Other Schools and Ours* (Holt, Rinehart & Winston, New York, rev. edn. 1963).

KLUCKHOHN, CLYDE, *Culture and Behaviour* (Free Press, Glencoe, 1962).

PRINCE MODUPE, *I Was a Savage* (Museum Press). An account of the traditional education of a West African.

It would be unreasonable to attempt to give here a reading list for education in every country in the world. The following should be consulted for the Swedish comparisons made in the text—

HUSÉN, TORSTEN and SVENSON, N. E., *Pedagogic Milieu and Development of Intellectual Skills* (*School Review*, Chicago, Spring, 1960).

ORRING, JONAS, *Comprehensive School and Continuation Schools in Sweden* (Kungl. Ecklesiastikdepartementet, Stockholm, 1962).

Appendix Five of the *Robbins Report* gives studies of Higher Education in a number of different countries, and there are numerous comparisons in Chapter V of the Report itself.

The *Year Books of Education*, produced by the London Institute of Education and Teachers College, Columbia (Evans Bros. and the World Book Co.) and devoted to a special topic each year, have a wealth of material about education in different countries.

E. *English Education Today*

Useful general books, though inevitably a little more out of date each year, are—

DENT, H. C., *The English Educational System* (Univ. of London Press, 1961).

LESTER-SMITH, W. O., *Education* (Penguin Books, 1961).

Indispensable are the following well-known Reports—

The Hadow Report, *The Education of the Adolescent* (H.M.S.O., 1926).

The Spens Report, *Report of the Consultative Committee on Secondary Education* (H.M.S.O., 1938).

The Norwood Report, *Curriculum and Examinations in Secondary Schools* (H.M.S.O., 1943).

The Fleming Report, *The Public Schools and the General Educational System* (H.M.S.O., 1944).

The Crowther Report, *15–18* 2 vols. (H.M.S.O., 1959).

The Newsom Report, *Half our Future* (H.M.S.O., 1963).

The Robbins Report, *Higher Education* Report appendices and evidence, Vols. 1–10 (H.M.S.O., 1963–4).

(The Plowden Report on the education of children from 5 to 13 is now in preparation.)

The following books may be noted as dealing with, or touching on, questions referred to in the text—

ASHBY, ERIC, *Technology and the Academics* (Macmillan, 1958).

BLISHEN, EDWARD, *Roaring Boy* (Thames & Hudson, 1955).

COLE, ROGER, *Comprehensive Schools in Action* (Oldbourne, 1964).

CROSLAND, C. A. R., *The Future of Socialism* (Cape, 1956).

CROSLAND, C. A. R., *Some Thoughts on English Education* (including a memorandum on Public schools as Sixth-Form Colleges by John Vaizey), in *Encounter*, Vol. 17, 1961.

DANCY, JOHN, *The Public Schools and the Future* (Faber, 1963).

FARLEY, RICHARD, *Secondary Modern Discipline* (A. &. C. Black, 1960).

JACKSON, B. and MARSDEN, D., *Education and the Working Class* (Routledge & Kegan Paul, 1962).

JACKSON, BRYAN, *Streaming* (Routledge & Kegan Paul, 1964).

LINSTEAD, PATRICK, (ed.), *The Complete Scientist* (Oxford, 1961).

LOUKES, HAROLD, *Secondary Modern* (Harrap, 1956).

MILLER, T. W. G., *Values in the Comprehensive School* (Oliver & Boyd, 1961).

NEWSOME, DAVID, *Godliness and Good Learning* (John Murray, 1961).

PEDLEY, ROBIN, *The Comprehensive School* (Penguin Books, 1953).

ROWE, A. W., *The Education of the Average Child* (Harrap, 1959).

TAYLOR, WILLIAM, *The Secondary Modern School* (Faber, 1963).

THE SCHOOLMASTER PUB. CO., *Inside the Comprehensive School* (1956).

VAIZEY, JOHN, Chapter on "The Public Schools" in *The Establishment* (Blond, 1959).

WILKINSON, RUPERT, *The Prefects* (Oxford University Press, 1962).

WILSON, JOHN, *Public Schools and Private Practice* (Allen & Unwin, 1962).